D1272068

RELIGIONS OF THE WORLD

BUDDHISM

CHRISTIANITY

CONFUCIANISM

HINDUISM

INDIGENOUS RELIGIONS

ISLAM

JUDAISM

NEW RELIGIONS

SHINTO

SIKHISM

TAOISM

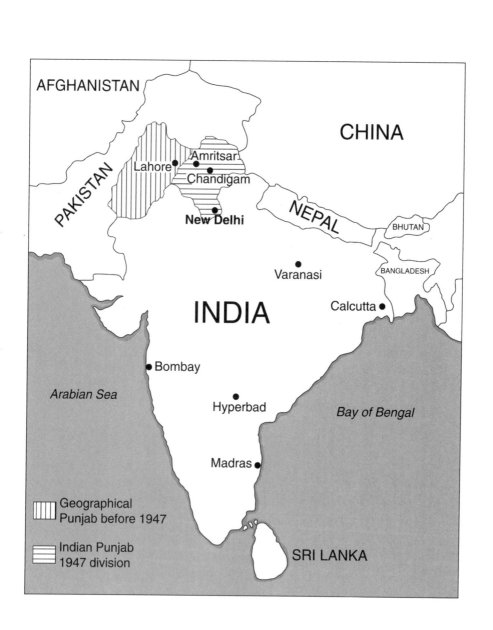

AFGHANISTAN

CHINA

PAKISTAN

Lahore • • Amritsar
          • Chandigam

New Delhi •

NEPAL

BHUTAN

BANGLADESH

• Varanasi

INDIA

Calcutta •

• Bombay

Arabian Sea

• Hyperbad

Bay of Bengal

Madras •

Geographical
Punjab before 1947

Indian Punjab
1947 division

SRI LANKA

RELIGIONS
OF THE
WORLD

SIKHISM

Sewa Singh Kalsi
Department of Theology
and Religious Studies,
University of Leeds

Series Consulting Editor Ann Marie B. Bahr
Professor of Religious Studies,
South Dakota State University

Foreword by Martin E. Marty
Professor Emeritus,
University of Chicago Divinity School

CHELSEA HOUSE
PUBLISHERS
A Haights Cross Communications Company ®
Philadelphia

FRONTIS: Sikhism was founded in the Punjab region of India in the late fifteenth century. In 1947, the Punjab was divided into Pakistan and India, the divisions of which are shown on this map. Today, the Punjab remains the only Indian state where Sikhs constitute a majority of the population.

CHELSEA HOUSE PUBLISHERS

VP, NEW PRODUCT DEVELOPMENT Sally Cheney
DIRECTOR OF PRODUCTION Kim Shinners
CREATIVE MANAGER Takeshi Takahashi
MANUFACTURING MANAGER Diann Grasse

Staff for SIKHISM

EXECUTIVE EDITOR Lee Marcott
EDITOR Christian Green
PRODUCTION EDITOR Noelle Nardone
PHOTO EDITOR Sarah Bloom
SERIES AND COVER DESIGNER Keith Trego
LAYOUT 21st Century Publishing and Communications, Inc.

A Haights Cross Communications ⏐ Company ®

www.chelseahouse.com

First Printing

9 8 7 6 5 4 3 2 1

Library of Congress Cataloging-in-Publication Data

Kalsi, Sewa Singh.
   Sikhism / Sewa Singh Kalsi.
      p. cm.—(Religions of the world)
   Includes bibliographical references and index.
   ISBN 0-7910-8098-6 (hardcover)—ISBN 0-7910-8356-X (pbk.)
   1. Sikhism. I. Title. II. Series.
BL2018.K255 2005
294.6—dc22

                                        2005002442

All links and web addresses were checked and verified to be correct at the time of publication. Because of the dynamic nature of the web, some addresses and links may have changed since publication and may no longer be valid.

CONTENTS

Foreword

Martin E. Marty

On this very day, like all other days, hundreds of millions of people around the world will turn to religion for various purposes.

On the one hand, there are purposes that believers in any or all faiths, as well as unbelievers, might regard as positive and benign. People turn to religion or, better, to their own particular faith, for the experience of healing and to inspire acts of peacemaking. They want to make sense of a world that can all too easily overwhelm them because it so often seems to be meaningless and even absurd. Religion then provides them with beauty, inspires their souls, and impels them to engage in acts of justice and mercy.

To be informed citizens of our world, readers have good reason to learn about these features of religions that mean so much to so many. Those who study the faiths do not have to agree with any of them and could not agree with all of them, different as they are. But they need basic knowledge of religions to understand other people and to work out strategies for living with them.

On the other hand—and religions always have an "other hand"—believers in any of the faiths, and even unbelievers who are against all of them, will find their fellow humans turning to their religions for purposes that seem to contradict all those positive features. Just as religious people can heal and be healed, they can also kill or be killed in the name of faith. So it has been through history.

This killing can be literal: Most armed conflicts and much terrorism today are inspired by the stories, commands, and promises that come along with various faiths. People can and do read and act upon scriptures that can breed prejudice and that lead them to reject other beliefs and believers. Or the killing can be figurative, which means that faiths can be deadening to the spirit. In the name of faith, many people are repressed, oppressed, sometimes victimized and abused.

If religion can be dangerous and if it may then come with "Handle with Care" labels, people who care for their own security, who want to lessen tensions and inspire concord, have to equip themselves by learning something about the scriptures and stories of their own and other faiths. And if they simply want to take delight in human varieties and imaginings, they will find plenty to please them in lively and reliable accounts of faiths.

A glance at television or at newspapers and magazines on almost any day will reveal stories that display one or both sides of religion. However, these stories usually have to share space with so many competing accounts, for example, of sports and enter-tainment or business and science, that writers and broadcasters can rarely provide background while writing headlines. Without such background, it is hard to make informed judgments.

The series RELIGIONS OF THE WORLD is designed to provide not only background but also rich illustrative material about the foreground, presenting the many features of faiths that are close at hand. Whoever reads all the volumes in the series will find that these religions have some elements in common. Overall, one can deduce that their followers take certain things with ultimate seriousness: human dignity, devotion to the sacred, the impulse to live a moral life. Yet few people are inspired by religions in general. They draw strength from what they hold particularly. These particulars of each faith are not always contradictory to those of others, but they are different in important ways. It is simply a fact that believers are informed and inspired by stories told in separate and special ways.

A picture might make all this vivid: Reading about a religion, visiting a place of worship, or coming into the company of those who believe in and belong to a particular faith, is like entering a room. Religions are, in a sense, spiritual "furnished apartments." Their adherents have placed certain pictures on the wall and moved in with their own kind of furnishings, having developed their special ways of receiving or blocking out light from such places. Some of their figurative apartments are airy, and some stress strength and security.

Philosopher George Santayana once wrote that, just as we do not speak language, we speak particular languages, so we have religion not as a whole but as religions "in particular." The power of each living and healthy religion, he added, consists in "its special and surprising message and in the bias which that revelation gives to life." Each creates "another world to live in."

The volumes in this series are introductions to several spiritual furnished apartments, guides to the special and surprising messages of these large and complex communities of faith, or religions. These are not presented as a set of items in a cafeteria line down which samplers walk, tasting this, rejecting that, and moving on. They are not bids for window-shoppers or shoppers of any sort, though it may be that a person without faith might be drawn to one or another expression of the religions here described. The real intention of the series is to educate.

Education could be dull and drab. Picture a boring professor standing in front of a class and droning on about distant realities. The authors in this series, however, were chosen because they can bring readers up close to faiths and, sometimes better, to people of faith; not to religion but to people who are religious in particular ways.

As one walks the streets of a great metropolis, it is not easy and may not even be possible to deduce the faith-commitments of those one passes unless they wear a particular costume—some garb or symbol prescribed by their faith. Therefore, while passing them by, it is not likely that one can learn much about the dreams and hopes, the fears and intentions, of those around them.

These books, in effect, stop the procession of passersby and bid visitors to enter those sanctuaries where communities worship. Each book could serve as a guide to worship. Several years ago, a book called *How to Be a Perfect Stranger* offered brief counsel on how to feel and to be at home among worshipers from other traditions. This series recognizes that we are not strangers to each other only in sanctuaries. We carry over our attachments to conflicting faiths where we go to work or vote or serve in the military or have fun. These "carryovers" tend to come from the basic stories and messages of the several faiths.

The publishers have taken great pains to assign their work to authors of a particular sort. Had these been anti-religious or anti–the religion about which they write, they would have done a disservice. They would, in effect, have been blocking the figurative doors to the faiths or smashing the furniture in the sanctuaries. On the other hand, it would be wearying and distorting had the assignment gone to public relations agents, advertisers who felt called to claim "We're Number One!" concerning the faith about which they write.

Fair-mindedness and accuracy are the two main marks of these authors. In rather short compass, they reach a wide range of subjects, focusing on everything one needs to advance basic understanding. Their books are like mini-encyclopedias, full of information. They introduce the holidays that draw some neighbors to be absent from work or school for a day or a season. They include galleries of notable figures in each faith-community.

Since most religions in the course of history develop different ways in the many diverse places where they thrive, or because they attract intelligent, strong-willed leaders and writers, they come up with different emphases. They divide and split off into numberless smaller groups: Protestant and Catholic and Orthodox Christians, Shiite and Sunni Muslims, Orthodox and Reform Jews, and many kinds of Buddhists and Hindus. The writers in this series do justice to these variations, providing a kind of map without which one will get lost in the effort to understand.

Some years ago, a rabbi friend, Samuel Sandmel, wrote a book about his faith called *The Enjoyment of Scripture*. What an astonishing concept, some might think: After all, religious scriptures deal with desperately urgent, life-and-death-and-eternity issues. They have to be grim and those who read them likewise. Not so. Sandmel knew what the authors of this series also know and impart: The journeys of faith and the encounter with the religions of others include pleasing and challenging surprises. I picture many a reader coming across something on these pages that at first looks obscure or forbidding, but then, after a slightly longer look, makes sense and inspires an "aha!" There are many occasions for "aha-ing!" in these books. One can also wager that many a reader will come away from the encounters thinking, "I never knew that!" or "I never thought of that before." And they will be more ready than they had been to meet strangers of other faiths in a world that so many faiths *have* to share, or that they *get* to share.

Martin E. Marty
The University of Chicago

Preface

Ann Marie B. Bahr

The majority of people, both in the United States and around the world, consider religion to be an important part of their lives. Beyond its significance in individual lives, religion also plays an important role in war and peace, politics, social policy, ethics, and cultural expression. Yet few people feel well-prepared to carry on a conversation about religion with friends, colleagues, or their congressional delegation. The amount of knowledge people have about their own faith varies, but very few can lay claim to a solid understanding of a religion other than their own. As the world is drawn closer together by modern communications, and the religions of the world jostle each other in religiously plural societies, the lack of our ability to dialogue about this aspect of our lives results in intercultural conflict rather than cooperation. It means that individuals of different religious persuasions will either fight about their faiths or avoid the topic of religion altogether. Neither of these responses aids in the building of healthy, religiously plural societies. This gap in our knowledge is therefore significant, and grows increasingly more significant as religion plays a larger role in national and international politics.

The authors and editors of this series are dedicated to the task of helping to prepare present and future decision-makers to deal with religious pluralism in a healthy way. The objective scholarship found in these volumes will blunt the persuasive power of popular misinformation. The time is short, however. Even now, nations are dividing along religious lines, and "neutral" states as well as partisan religious organizations are precariously, if not always intentionally, tipping delicate balances of power in favor of one religious group or another with doles of aid and support for certain policies or political leaders. Intervention in the affairs of other nations is always a risky business, but doing it without understanding of the religious sensitivities of the populace dramatically increases the chances that even well-intentioned intervention will be perceived as political coercion or cultural invasion. With such signs of ignorance already manifest, the day of reckoning for educational policies that ignore the study of the world's religions cannot be far off.

This series is designed to bring religious studies scholarship to the leaders of today and tomorrow. It aims to answer the questions that students, educators, policymakers, parents, and citizens might have about the new religious milieu in which we find ourselves. For example, a person hearing about a religion that is foreign to him or her might want answers to questions like these:

- How many people believe in this religion? What is its geographic distribution? When, where, and how did it originate?

- What are its beliefs and teachings? How do believers worship or otherwise practice their faith?

- What are the primary means of social reinforcement? How do believers educate their youth? What are their most important communal celebrations?

- What are the cultural expressions of this religion? Has it inspired certain styles of art, architecture, literature, or music? Conversely, does it avoid art, literature, or music for religious reasons? Is it associated with elements of popular culture?

- How do the people who belong to this religion remember the past? What have been the most significant moments in their history?

- What are the most salient features of this religion today? What is likely to be its future?

We have attempted to provide as broad coverage as possible of the various religious forces currently shaping the planet. Judaism, Christianity, Islam, Hinduism, Buddhism, Confucianism, Taoism, Sikhism, and Shinto have each been allocated an entire volume. In recognition of the fact that many smaller ancient and new traditions also exercise global influence, we present coverage of some of these in two additional volumes titled "Indigenous Religions" and "New Religions." Each volume in the series discusses demographics and geography, founder or foundational period, scriptures, worldview, worship or practice, growing up in the religion, cultural expressions, calendar and holidays, history, and the religion in the world today.

The books in this series are written by scholars. Their approach to their subject matter is neutral and objective. They are not trying to convert readers to the religion they are describing. Most scholars, however, value the religion they have chosen to study, so you can expect the general tone of these books to be appreciative rather than critical.

Religious studies scholars are experts in their field, but they are not critics in the same sense in which one might be an art, film, or literary critic. Religious studies scholars feel obligated to describe a tradition faithfully and accurately, and to interpret it in a way that will allow nonbelievers as well as believers to grasp its essential structure, but they do not feel compelled to pass judgment on it. Their goal is to increase knowledge and understanding.

Academic writing has a reputation for being dry and uninspiring. If so, religious studies scholarship is an exception. Scholars of religion have the happy task of describing the words and deeds of some of the world's most amazing people: founders, prophets, sages, saints, martyrs, and bodhisattvas.

The power of religion moves us. Today, as in centuries past, people thrill to the ethical vision of Confucianism, or the dancing beauty of Hinduism's images of the divine. They are challenged by the one, holy God of the Jews, and comforted by the saving promise of Christianity. They are inspired by the stark purity of

Islam, by the resilience of tribal religions, by the energy and innovation of the new religions. The religions have retained such a strong hold on so many people's lives over such a long period of time largely because they are unforgettable.

Religious ideas, institutions, and professions are among the oldest in humanity's history. They have outlasted the world's great empires. Their authority and influence have endured far beyond that of Earth's greatest philosophers, military leaders, social engineers, or politicians. It is this that makes them so attractive to those who seek power and influence, whether such people intend to use their power and influence for good or evil. Unfortunately, in the hands of the wrong person, religious ideas might as easily be responsible for the destruction of the world as for its salvation. All that stands between us and that outcome is the knowledge of the general populace. In this as in any other field, people must be able to critically assess what they are being told.

The authors and editors of this series hope that all who seek to wield the tremendous powers of religion will do so with unselfish and noble intent. Knowing how unlikely it is that that will always be the case, we seek to provide the basic knowledge necessary to critically assess the degree to which contemporary religious claims are congruent with the history, scriptures, and genius of the traditions they are supposed to represent.

Ann Marie B. Bahr
South Dakota State University

1

Introduction

Realization of Truth is higher than all else.
Higher still is Truthful Living.

—Guru Nanak, Sri Rag

What is Sikhism? Who are the Sikhs? These may appear to be simple questions but they are in fact rather complex and quite problematic to answer. The term *Sikhism* has two components: "Sikh" and "ism." The word *Sikh* is the Punjabi form of the Sanskrit word *shishya*, which means "student," a learner or a disciple, while "ism" is a Greek suffix that was added to the word "Sikh" around 1830 by the British administrators who ruled India at the time to denote the Sikh tradition. The Sikhs apply the terms *Gur/u-mat*, Sikh *dharm/a*, and *Sikhi* to describe the concept of "Sikh tradition"; *Gur/u-mat* (literally, guru's intention) denotes the teachings of gurus; Sikh *dharm/a* means religious, social, and moral obligations as prescribed in Sikh scriptures; and *Sikhi* denotes the Sikh way of life based on the teachings of Sikh gurus.

Sikhism is primarily a Punjabi tradition that originated and developed under the leadership of the ten human Gurus. Like most Indic traditions, such as Hinduism, Buddhism, and Jainism, the Sikh tradition is a *guru-sikh* (teacher-disciple)-oriented movement in which the relationship between a *guru* and his/her disciple is considered sacred. The term *guru* is derived from the Sanskrit language and denotes a teacher, an enlightener, or a spiritual guide. A *guru* is perceived as a divinely endowed person who guides his/her disciples in every sphere of life.

The followers of Sikh tradition are popularly known as Sikhs. It is a common perception that male Sikhs are easily recognizable by their turbans and beards. But many Hindu and Muslim men also wear turbans in the subcontinent of India; in fact, the turban is an important article of daily dress for many Muslim men in Arab countries. It is noteworthy that many Sikh men and nearly all Sikh women only wear turbans in public. Thus the criterion for wearing a turban does not provide a complete answer for defining Sikh identity. Second, it is assumed that all male Sikhs have "Singh" as their surname. Ironically, a significant number of Hindus in India belong to the *Kashatriya* (warrior and princely) caste and bear the surname "Singh."

Let us proceed to unlock the mystery of the term *Sikh* as applied to a significant section of Punjabi society and members of 3HO (American Sikh converts). To find answers for our query, we ought to begin with the founder of the Sikh movement, Nanak Dev, popularly known as Guru Nanak. He was born into a Hindu *Khatri*-caste (merchants) household in 1469 in the Punjab. His father was a revenue officer. He was privileged to be educated in both the Sanskrit and Persian languages. From a very young age he is believed to have had a deep interest in understanding the meaning and purpose of life. Although he enjoyed the company of wandering Hindu saints and Sufi leaders of Islam, he was deeply distressed by the caste divisions within Punjabi/Indic society and was highly critical of the leaders of the Hindu hierarchy who justified the caste system as part of the divine order.

Guru Nanak intensely believed in the oneness of God. His search for truth resulted in a divine calling at Sultanpur, where he made his historic declaration: "There is no Hindu and there is no Muslim." Soon thereafter he undertook long journeys in India and abroad and visited important centers of Hindu and Muslim pilgrimage, where he met many religious leaders. After his travels, Guru Nanak settled at Kartarpur, where he began to share his understanding of divine truth with people who became his disciples. They were popularly known as *Nanak-panthis* (literally, followers of Nanak's path or teachings). This is how the title "*Nanak-panthi*" originated and became popular among Punjabis.

The Sikh movement has passed through many stages. In the first phase (1469–1606), Guru Nanak and his four successors established some of the fundamental institutions of Sikh tradition, that is, the institution of human *guruship*, congregational worship, the *langar* (communal meal), compilation of the *Adi Granth* (Sikh scripture), and the Golden Temple. The second phase (1606–1675) began with the martyrdom of the fifth Guru, Arjun Dev. He was succeeded by his son, Hargobind, who adopted a radical policy of *miri-piri* (temporal and spiritual authority) for the defense of the Sikh community. It is believed that he trained his followers in martial arts and fought battles against the Mughal army. During his ministry, we first come across the use of the corporate title of "Sikh" for the Guru's followers.

The martyrdom of the ninth Guru, Teg Bahadur, may be described as the dawn of the third phase. He was succeeded by his son, the tenth Guru, Gobind Singh, who founded a radical institution called the *Khalsa* in 1699. Guru Gobind Singh introduced some fundamental innovations: a) institution of the *panj pyarey* (the five beloved ones); b) new-style initiation ceremony of *amrit* (water of immortality); c) and introduction of the title of *Singh* for men and *Kaur* for women. The distinction between *amritdhari* (initiated) and non-*amritdhari* Sikhs occurred after the founding of the *Khalsa* in 1699.

Amritdhari Sikhs: A Sikh who has been initiated according to the new-style initiation ceremony of *amrit* is called an *amritdhari*. The wearing of five emblems is mandatory for an *amritdhari* Sikh:

1) *kes* (uncut hair)

2) *kangha* (a small wooden comb worn in the hair)

3) *kirpan* (a sword; today, a small sword is worn by initiated Sikhs)

4) *kachha/kachhahira* (a pair of knee-length pants)

5) *kara* (a steel bracelet/circle worn on the right wrist)

Non*amritdhari* Sikhs: The category of non*amritdhari* Sikhs comprises *kesdhari* and non*kesdhari* Sikhs, who are popularly called *mona* (clean-shaven) Sikhs.

Kesdhari Sikhs: A Sikh person who keeps his/her hair unshorn and observes a prescribed code of discipline, except for the initiation ritual, is known as *kesdhari*. It is important to note that all *amritdhari* Sikhs are *kesdhari*, whereas *kesdhari* may not be *amritdhari*. The distinguishing feature between the two identities is the *amrit* (initiation) ceremony, which requires wearing of the five emblems of the *Khalsa*.

Sahajdhari Sikhs: The term *sahajdhari* is applied to non*amrit-dhari* Sikhs, which includes *kesdhari* and clean-shaven (*mona*) Sikhs. The word *sahaj* means "slow" or "natural" and the term *sahajdhari* denotes a "slow adopter," or a Sikh who is preparing him/herself to become *amritdhari*. Defining Sikh identity is complex and problematic. Originally, people chose to enter the Sikh *Panth*, but nowadays children born into Sikh families are regarded as Sikhs and usually have "Singh" or "Kaur" as surnames; and this includes clean-shaven Sikhs.

Sikh Gurus applied the term *Sikh* to their disciples (sometimes they used the term *gursikh*, meaning guru-oriented). Sikh preachers and *ragis* (religious musicians) reverentially address members of the congregation as *gusikh*. Let us look at the definitions of a Sikh person—one from the Adi Granth and another from the Sikh *Rahit Maryada* (the Sikh code of discipline, a guide to the Sikh way of life), approved by the *Shiromani Gurdwara Parbandhak Committee* (Supreme Management Committee of Gurdwaras) and constituted under the Punjab Gurdwara Act of 1925:

1) "He who calls himself a Sikh of the True Guru, he should get up in the early hours of the morning and remember the Name of the Lord ... Then when the day dawns, he should sing the *bani* (compositions) of the Guru and remember the Name of the Lord with every breath ... I beg for the dust of the feet of that *Gursikh* who not only repeat the Name of the Lord but also makes others to repeat it."[1]

2) "A Sikh is any person whose faith is in one God, the Ten Gurus and their teachings, and the Adi Granth. In addition, he or she must believe in the necessity and importance of *amrit* (initiation) and must not adhere to any other religion."[2]

It is important to note that the second definition does not make any distinction between a *kesdhari*, an *amritdhari*, or a *sahajdhari* Sikh. Although the definition of a Sikh in the *Rahit Maryada* applies to the overwhelming majority of Sikhs, it does not include those who believe in the tradition of a living guru like the Namdhari Sikhs.

PUNJABI HERITAGE
The Indus Valley civilization is regarded as one of the oldest civilizations in the world, and its cradle was the soil of the Punjab. The literal meaning of the Persian term *panj-ab* is "five waters," which denotes the land of five rivers. The present state of the Punjab was divided between India and Pakistan in 1947. The term *panj-ab* was not meant to be taken literally, because its boundaries have been changing along with the political changes occurring in India. For example, the British Punjab comprised the entire plain between the rivers Jamuna and Indus. The Punjab region is a geographical entity of its own. The Himalaya Mountains stand to its north, while its southern boundary is marked by the Thar Desert.

The Himalayas comprise one of the outstanding features of the geography of the Punjab and India. The three river systems of the Indus, Ganges, and Brahmaputra, on which the life of the subcontinent of India depends, originate in the Himalayas. As a geographical region, its climate can be divided into four seasons. The rains of July and August mark the end of the extreme heat of May and June, and the return of spring in March and April marks the end of the extreme cold of December and January. The most temperate times come in February–March and October–November.

The most significant factors in the development of the Indus Valley civilization were undoubtedly its fertile soil and its rivers (Indus, Jehlum, Chenab, Ravi, Sutlej, and Beas), which provided a constant supply of water for irrigation and development of agriculture. Towns and village communities grew up in the river valleys and transformed the region into a seat of civilization now popularly known as the Indus Valley civilization. It was a highly developed urban society with such cities as Mohenjo-Daro and Harappa, important centers of trade and sociocultural life, with multistory buildings and advanced drainage systems, which demonstrates the quality of life the people of the Indus Valley culture enjoyed.

These people developed an elaborate agricultural system and a rural economy based on villages that supplied the daily needs of an urban society. A new class of craftsmen, including carpenters, blacksmiths, and tanners, arose to manufacture and repair agricultural implements. Interestingly, the Indus Valley culture had already spread over a very large area, including present-day Punjab. This region began to be known as *Aryavarat* (literally, land of the Arya people) after the development of Vedic culture. For many centuries it was known as *Bharat Varsh*. The origin of the name *Bharat Varsh* can be traced to the Hindu deity Lord Rama's half-brother, Bharat, who looked after Rama's kingdom during his exile.

The term *Bharat* has been adopted by the people of India to indicate their mother land. Many Indians reverentially use the term *Bharat Mata* to mean "Mother India." India was called *Hindostan* by its Muslim invaders, a term composed of two words: *Hindo/u* and *stan*. The origin of the "Hindo/u" is most interesting. The river Indus is called "Sindhu" in Sanskrit. The outsiders called the people around and beyond the river Sindh "Sindhus." "Stan" is from the Persian for residence or locality. Thus, the term *Sindh* gradually changed into *Hind* and the land conquered by the Muslim rulers began to be called Hindostan (literally, the home of Hindu people). The term *Hindu* had no religious connotation as understood in today's world. Interestingly, there are a number of Punjabi/Sikh clans who are called Sindhus. The Greeks gave the name *Indos* to the river Sindh and *India* to the country through which it flowed.

The arrival of the Aryan people from the west into the Punjab, around 1500 B.C.E., had a dramatic impact on Punjabi society. Social interaction between the Aryans and the indigenous people resulted in a new culture and a specialized social structure that is popularly called the caste system. The Vedas and other great works of the Sanskrit language were written in the Punjab.

After the Aryans, numerous invaders—including Greeks, Turks, and Mughals—entered India through the Punjab and left a cultural mark on Punjabi identity. For example, the Urdu language evolved and developed under the umbrella of social interaction between Persian soldiers and Punjabi people. It is believed that Guru Nanak witnessed the slaughter of ordinary Punjabi people by the Mughal army at Aimnabad in 1526. Commenting upon the social and political degeneration of the society at that time, Guru Nanak said, "Kings are butchers; cruelty is their weapon. The sense of duty has taken wings and vanished. Falsehood reigns over the land as a veil of darkness."

Ironically, Mughal rule in India contributed significantly to the development of the Sikh tradition and its principal institutions. The interaction between Hinduism and Islam had a major impact on the development of Sikh tradition.

MAJOR SIKH SECTS

The death of the tenth Guru, Gobind Singh, in 1708, resulted in an unprecedented change within the Sikh movement. In 1710, Sikhs established a sovereign state in the Punjab under the leadership of Banda Bahadur. Although Banda's rule lasted for only six years, it paved the way for the establishment of a Punjabi/Sikh state under the leadership of Maharaja Ranjit Singh in 1799. The Sikh raj lasted for fifty years, until the annexation of the Punjab by the British in 1849.

This fifty-year period of independence brought peace and prosperity to the Punjab, and the Sikh hierarchy became enormously wealthy. One consequence was that some Sikhs lapsed into traditional ritualistic practices, while some converted to Christianity. Several of Maharaja Ranjit Singh's wives committed *suttee* by throwing themselves on his burning funeral pyre. There was in fact no central authority within the Sikh movement, which resulted in the birth of a number of reform movements.

Namdhari Sikhs

The term *Namdhari* is composed of two words: *Nam* and *dhari*. *Nam* means God's name and *dhari* denotes an adopter, so Namdhari literally means one who upholds the name of God. The Namdhari movement was founded by *Baba* Balak Singh (1797–1862). As his successor he appointed Ram Singh, who transformed the movement into a dynamic sociopolitical force within the Punjab. The Namdhari movement also played an important role in the struggle for Indian independence. In 1872, the British government deported Ram Singh to Burma for causing unrest in the Punjab and sixty-six Namdhari Sikhs were executed when they were tied to the mouths of cannons.

Let us examine some of the distinctive features of the Namdhari Sikh movement:

1) According to Namdhari tradition, the tenth Guru, Gobind Singh, did not die at Nanded in 1708 but continued his mission under the name of Ajapal Singh and appointed Balak Singh his successor.

2) Namdhari Sikhs believe in the continuity of the line of human gurus, although they have a very high regard for the *Guru Granth Sahib*. They also believe that their leader, Guru Ram Singh, is still alive and will return one day to lead them.

3) All Namdhari Sikhs are *amritdhari* (initiated Sikhs). They wear white clothes and are strict vegetarians. The style of their turban is called *sidhi-pagri* (laid flat at the forehead).

4) Namdhari Sikhs practice the system of arranged marriage, but they prefer to choose spouses from Namdhari families.

5) At a Namdhari wedding, the bride and groom walk around the *havan* (holy fire) while *lavan* (wedding

hymns) are recited from the Adi Granth. Namdhari brides do not cover their faces. Before the wedding ceremony, the bride and groom are initiated according to Namdhari tradition.

6) The headquarters of the Namdhari movement is located at Bhaini Sahib, the birthplace of Guru Ram Singh.

7) Namdhari Sikhs use a woolen rosary (*mala*) during *nam-simran* (meditating on God's name) sessions.

8) Namdhari Sikhs do not fly the *nishan-sahib* (Sikh flag) over their *gurdwaras* (place of worship).

Namdhari Sikhs have established their gurdwaras in many countries. Their present leader, Satguru Jagjit Singh, regularly visits his followers abroad. A Namdhari service begins early in the morning, following the tradition of Gurdwara Hazzor Sahib, where the tenth Guru, Gobind Singh, had died.

Nirankari Sikhs
The Nirankari movement was founded by Baba Dyal Das during the period of Sikh rule in the Punjab. Nirankari translates to "one who believes in a formless God." Baba Dyal Das was born in 1783 and died in 1854. He had witnessed the gradual process of ritualism creeping into the observances of Sikh practitioners, who, according to Baba Dyal Das, had forgotten the teachings of Guru Nanak. He preached purification of Sikh practices and insisted upon righteous conduct rather than meaningless ritual.

Baba Dyal Das made a significant contribution to simplification of the Sikh rites of passage. Nirankari Sikhs consistently campaigned for the right to solemnize the Sikh wedding in the presence of the Adi Granth and recital of *lavan*. Nirankaris also believe in the necessity of a human guru.

The Radhasoami Movement

The Radhasoami movement is popularly called the Radhasoami *Satsang* (True Association of the Lord of the Soul). The term *Radhasoami* is composed of two words: *Radha* and *Soami*— Radha was the favorite *gopi* (cowgirl) of the Hindu god Krishna and *Soami* literally means Lord. The term *Radha* symbolizes Lord Krishna's soul. Radhasoami devotees perceive themselves as the "Soul of the Lord (God)." The founder of the Radhasoami movement was Baba Shiv Dyal, who was popularly known as *Soamiji*. He was born in 1818 and died in 1878. He was greatly influenced by the teachings of the Adi Granth. The Radhasoami movement attracted a large number of Sikhs when Jaimal Singh, a disciple of Baba Shiv Dyal, established his headquarters at Beas in the Punjab.

Radhasoamis believe in a living guru who is believed to have been brought into human form to give *Nam* (God's name) and to lead properly prepared devotees back to their *sach-khand* (true home). They do not install the Adi Granth or any other scriptures at their place of worship. At their service, called a satsang, the guru sits on a raised platform and preaches from a selection of hymns taken from the Adi Granth as well as from compositions of other *sants* (holy men). Their teachings are strictly anticaste, and the movement has attracted a large number of untouchables (people of low status in the Hindu caste system). In the diaspora, they have attracted many members of other ethnic groups for whom the *satsang* is conducted in English.

Radhasoamis are strict vegetarians. They do not distribute *karah-parshad* (sanctified food) at the culmination of their *satsang* sessions, and they do not insist on covering the head or removing shoes. Since their guru lives at the *dera* (headquarters), in Beas, it has become an important center of Radhasoami pilgrimage. They have built a modern hospital in Beas, where a number of overseas Radhasoami doctors provide free service for a couple of weeks every year. The movement has attracted a significant number of educated people, who are mainly responsible for overall management of the movement.

The 3HO Sikhs

One of the most significant developments within the Sikh diaspora is the unprecedented conversion of a large number of American citizens (including blacks, whites, and Hispanics). They are popularly known as members of the Sikh Dharma Brotherhood. The term *3HO* stands for "Healthy, Happy, Holy Organization" and was founded in 1971 by a Punjabi Sikh, Harbhajan Singh Puri—popularly known as *Yogi* Bhajan (who passed away in October 2004)—a charismatic leader who attracted a large number of white Americans to Sikhism. They claim to have more than one hundred centers in North America that serve over 250,000 3HO members.

All members of the Sikh Dharma Brotherhood are *amritdhari*. They follow the *Khalsa* code of discipline very strictly. Both men and women wear turbans, and they usually wear white clothes. They are strict vegetarians and do not permit the use of alcohol or other intoxicants. In fact, they claim to have modeled their lifestyle according to the teachings of Sikh Gurus. Their *gurdwaras* run *Yoga* schools, where they teach Punjabi, *shabad-kirtan* (religious singing), and such musical instruments as the *tablas* (a pair of drums) and harmonium to their youngsters.

A group of white American Sikh *ragis* used to accompany their leader, Yogi Bhajan, whenever he traveled abroad, and they would perform *shabad-kirtan* at local gurdwaras. In 1996, a group of 3HO women participated in *shabad-kirtan* at the Golden Temple, in Amritsar, India, which provoked strong objections within a segment of the Sikh community. Interestingly, the controversy was resolved by the Shiromani Gurdwara Parbandhak Committee, who endorsed the principle that women could perform all types of *sewa* (voluntary service), including *shabad-kirtan* in the Golden Temple.

Although Punjabi Sikhs admire their dedication and commitment to Sikh teachings, they still call them *gora* (white) Sikhs. White American Sikh converts challenge the religious identity of Punjabi Sikhs who drink alcohol, eat meat, trim beards, and are clean-shaven. They hold that one "can be a Punjabi no matter what you do and no matter where you go, but you cannot call yourself a Sikh unless you are living as a practicing, religious Sikh."[3]

SIKH POPULATION

Although Sikhs make up less than 2 percent of the population of India, their impact on the religious, social, economic, and political institutions of modern India is far more significant than their numerical strength. The overwhelming proportion of Sikhs live in the Punjab, the only state in India where they form a majority —nearly 63 percent of the population. According to the 1991 national census of India, the Sikh population was as follows:

Punjab	Over 12 million
Other Parts of India	6 million
Outside India	2 million
Total Population	Over 20 million

It is important to note that according to the 2001 national census of India, the Sikh population of India was 19 million (1.9 percent of the total Indian population of 1.028 billion).

SIKH POPULATION IN THE DIASPORA

United Kingdom*	**336,000** (United Kingdom national census, 2001)
Canada	**278,415** (Canada national census, 2001)
United States	**234,000** (estimation)
Australia	**12,017** (Australia national census, 1999)
New Zealand	**2,814** (estimation)

* No figures are available for Sikhs living in continental Europe, although many European countries have small Sikh communities where they have established gurdwaras.

2

Founders

*Our service in the world gets us
a seat in the Court of the Lord.*

—Guru Nanak, Adi Granth

Originating in the Punjab during the fifteenth century, Sikhism is one of the youngest religious traditions in the world. As previously mentioned, Sikhism is similar to Buddhism, Hinduism, and Jainism in that it is centered around a *guru-sikh* (teacher-disciple) relationship between guru and disciple is regarded sacred. It is a remarkable story of a socioreligious movement which, under the creative leadership of ten human Gurus, developed into a well-organized force in the Punjab. Our quest for an understanding of the historical development of the Sikh tradition and an insight into Punjabi/Sikh culture must begin with a biographical sketch of its founder, Guru Nanak Dev, and his response to the religious, social, and political climate of fifteenth-century Punjab.

Guru Nanak was born in 1469 in a Punjabi village called Talwandi. By the time of his birth, India had been under Muslim rule for more than five hundred years. Islam, through the creative leadership of Sufi (Muslim) saints, had emerged as an important socioreligious component of Punjabi society. Guru Nanak grew up within a multifaith environment, which impacted greatly on his understanding of the oneness of God. Guru Nanak's father, Kalu, was a high-caste *Khatri*. He was literate in Persian, the official language of the state, and worked as a revenue collector for the government. According to Sikh tradition, Guru Nanak learned Sanskrit and Persian at his village school.

From a very young age, Nanak is believed to have had a craving for answers to the meaning and purpose of human existence. Thus, he was very interested in the company of wandering Hindu saints, as well as Muslim holy men called *faqirs*. There are numerous stories about Guru Nanak's early life that Sikh parents tell their children. It is said that once Guru Nanak's father gave him some money to set up a business. While Nanak was on his way to a nearby town, he met a group of *sadhus* (wandering Hindu ascetics) and spent his money to feed the saints. His father angrily asked Nanak what he had done with the money, and Guru Nanak replied, "I made a *sacha sauda* [true bargain]; poor *sadhus* were hungry and I bought food for them."

Guru Nanak got married and had two children. He was sent to Sultanpur to find employment, where his brother-in-law had a job with the revenue department of the government. Soon Guru Nanak started working in a government store called a *modikhana*. Sultanpur, the seat of the regional government, was a thriving town. There Guru Nanak met a number of Hindu and Muslim scholars who engaged each other in debating their respective religious doctrines. His own search for truth resulted in a miraculous experience at Sultanpur.

DIVINE CALL

It is believed that Guru Nanak received a divine call at Sultanpur. One morning when he went to bathe in a nearby river, it is believed that he was taken into God's court. He reappeared after three days declaring, "There is no Hindu and there is no Muslim." His declaration focused on the unity and equality of humankind, transcending the sectarian boundaries of caste and religious bigotry.

Guru Nanak became thoroughly familiar with the social and political structure of Punjabi society. He was highly critical of the caste system and was deeply distressed by the social divisions in Punjabi/Indic society. He strongly denounced the hypocrisy of traditional Hindu leaders, saying, "Look at the behavior of the Hindu leaders; they wear Islamic dress on duty and eat Muslim food, but when they return home in the evening they change into their traditional Hindu dress, put a *tilak* (religious mark) on their forehead and smear the kitchen

GURU NANAK DEV ENUNCIATES HIS ATTITUDE ABOUT CASTE STATUS

Worthless is caste and worthless
an exalted name.
For all humankind there is
but a single refuge.*

* Adi Granth, 83.

with cow-dung for ritual purification and then recite Vedic hymns while cooking vegetarian food."[4]

Guru Nanak was a creative genius. He did not merely denounce and condemn the caste system and morally degrading customs and rituals. He took practical steps to translate his ideas and set out on a long journey through India and abroad with the purpose of visiting various centers of learning. He chose Mardana, a Muslim minstrel, as his companion—another expression of his understanding of the oneness of God.

During his travels, Guru Nanak wrote *bani* (spoken compositions) in poetic form in Punjabi, the language of the common people, rather than Sanskrit or Persian. He thereby removed the barrier between God and the people and released them from the clutches of religious zealots like the Brahmins (Hindu priests). As Guru Nanak composed poetry, Mardana set it to music and sang. Since then, the tradition of *shabad-kirtan* has become an integral part of the Sikh service.

The story of Guru Nanak's visit to Mecca is very popular among Sikhs. According to tradition, Guru Nanak and Mardana traveled to the Muslim holy city, and while there Guru Nanak slept with his feet facing a shrine. One of the custodians of the shrine could not believe his eyes and shouted at Guru Nanak for his un-Islamic behavior. Guru Nanak politely inquired, "What have I done?" to which the custodian replied, "You are sleeping with your feet towards the sacred house of God." Guru Nanak smiled and said, "Please turn my feet towards that direction where you think God does not exist." Listening to Guru Nanak's reply, the custodian became enlightened and asked for forgiveness. At another encounter in Mecca, Guru Nanak was asked who was superior, a Hindu or a Muslim, to which he replied that without good deeds both were living in darkness. He declared, "Truth is high but higher still is truthful living."

Guru Nanak strongly denounced ritualistic practices and condemned traditional leaders for their desire to keep ordinary people in the dark. On one occasion, he visited Hardwar, one of the ancient Hindu centers of pilgrimage, situated on the banks of the Ganges River. He stood with the pilgrims—who were praying while throwing water toward the rising sun—in the river for an early morning bath. Guru Nanak, however, began to throw water to the west. The people around him were surprised and alarmed to see someone acting against the centuries-old Hindu tradition of offering water to their ancestors.

Guru Nanak was summoned by the custodians of Hardwar to explain what he had been doing in the Ganges that morning. He replied that he was watering his fields in his village near Lahore. The Brahmins laughed at his answer and remarked, "Your water could not reach your fields in the Punjab, which are nearly two hundred miles away from Hardwar." "Well, then how far is the sun and your ancestors from Hardwar?" came the answer. They replied that the sun was millions and millions of miles from Earth. "If my water cannot reach my fields a couple hundred miles from Hardwar," responded Nanak, "how can your water possibly reach your ancestors and the god Sun which is so far from Earth?" The Brahmins were speechless before Guru Nanak, who had exposed the futility of their superstitious rituals.

Guru Nanak was a great traveler; he visited many important centers of Hindu and Muslim pilgrimage. He also collected the writings of Muslim and Hindu saints, some of whom were born in the lowest-caste groups, such as Kabir, Farid, and Ravidas. After more than twenty years of extensive travel, Guru Nanak returned to the Punjab and settled in Kartarpur (literally, God's village), a town he founded on the banks of the Ravi River. It was at Kartarpur where he began to give practical shape to his radical ideas. He launched a crusade against the caste divisions and declared that God had no caste. He despised the exclusion of low-caste people from entering and worshipping at Hindu temples. He introduced the traditions of *sangat* (communal worship) and *langar* (communal meal) to transmit the message of the oneness of God. He also preached the significance of *kirat-karna* (earning one's living through honest means) and *wand chhakna* (sharing the fruits of one's labor with others).

Soon Guru Nanak's house turned into a *dharmsala* (place of worship), where people of different castes and faiths would gather for *shabad-kirtan* and share a communal meal while sitting in rows, without any distinction of gender, caste, or status. Kartarpur became a very popular center and attracted large numbers of people who became Guru Nanak's disciples, known as *Nanakpanthees* (followers of Nanak's path).

Guru Nanak died in 1539 at Kartarpur. Before his death, he appointed Angad, a trusted disciple, as his successor, and gave him the collection of writings of other saints, as well as his own, for the spiritual nurturing of future generations.

Let us look at the mode of transfer of guruship to the second Guru, Angad Dev, whose previous name was Lehna. In order to avoid any opposition from his sons, Guru Nanak declared his preference for Lehna to be his successor in public: "You are Angad, a part of my body." The word *Angad* means a limb or part of the body. Before his death, Guru Nanak had one of his chief disciples, Bhai Buddha, daub Angad Dev's forehead with saffron and proclaimed him the second Guru. It is recorded in the Adi Granth that "Nanak proclaimed the accession of Lehna ... He [Lehna] had the same light and the same ways. The Guru merely changed his body." Guru Nanak's decision to choose his successor proved to be a most crucial step, one that laid the foundation of the institution of *guruship* in the Sikh tradition.

GURU NANAK'S SUCCESSORS

Guru Nanak was followed by nine guru successors, who also innovated and developed some of the fundamental institutions of Sikh tradition, such as the Golden Temple, the Sikh scriptures (Adi Granth), the place of worship (*gurdwara*), and the Sikh brotherhood (*Khalsa*). These institutions played a key role in shaping a distinctive Sikh movement.

Let us look to the post-Nanak period, which can be neatly divided into three main segments: 1) from the second Guru, Angad Dev, to the fifth Guru, Arjun Dev; 2) from the sixth

Guru, Hargobind, to the ninth Guru, Teg Bahadur, and, finally;
3) the ministry of the tenth Guru, Gobind Singh.

Guru Angad Dev (1504–1552)

Guru Angad Dev moved to the village of Khadur, where he
established his headquarters. He also composed *bani* like his
predecessor and included them in the collection he had received
from Guru Nanak. According to Sikh tradition, Guru Angad Dev
invented the Punjabi alphabet, which is popularly known as
Gurmukhi (from the guru's mouth). The Adi Granth is written
in *Gurmukhi* script. The institution of *langar* had become very
popular during this period, and it is believed that his wife, Khivi,
contributed enormously to management of the Guru's *langar*.

Guru Amar Das (1479–1574)

Before his death in 1552, Guru Angad Dev appointed Guru
Amar Das, who also received the collection of *bani* from his
predecessor, as his successor. By this time, the Sikh movement
had expanded enormously and new Sikh *sangats* had emerged
throughout the Punjab. Guru Amar Das appointed his deputies
to act on his behalf as preachers. Most importantly, he formalized
the tradition of *langar* by making it compulsory for everyone
who desired to visit the Guru; this made a strong contribution
to breaking down caste and gender divisions.

Guru Amar Das also encouraged his followers to gather at his
headquarters on the festivals of *Diwali* and *Baisakhi*. He also
dug a sacred well, called the *baoli*, at Goindwal, where pilgrims
still walk down a series of steps leading to the water for a ritual
bath. Interestingly, the *baoli* has eighty-four steps, symbolizing
the traditional belief in the concept of *chaurasi lakh joon*
(8,400,000 lives before one attains the human life).

Tradition has it that the Mughal emperor Akbar, a descendant of
Timur and Genghis Khan, once visited Goindwal, where he had to
dine with other pilgrims before being allowed to meet Guru Amar
Das. Akbar was very pleased with what he witnessed there, and
before he left he made a large grant of land to the Sikh community.

Guru Ram Das (1534–1581)

Before his death, Guru Amar Das appointed his son-in-law Guru Ram Das, the fourth Guru, who held the *guruship* for only seven years, as his successor. His first name was Jetha (literally, the first son). He was entrusted by Guru Amar Das to establish a new center at Ramdaspur, later known as Amritsar. Guru Ram Das is also responsible for excavating the sacred pool there. He appointed his youngest son, Arjun Dev, as his successor. Guru Ram Das' eldest son, Prithvi Chand, strongly disapproved of this decision and conspired against his brother.

Guru Arjun Dev (1563–1606)

Guru Arjun Dev took the leadership of the Sikh community at a most important period in the history of the Punjab. Guru Arjun Dev decided to collect the writings of his predecessors and set out to compile the Adi Granth, which he completed in 1604. His second mission was to build the Golden Temple at Amritsar. Guru Arjun Dev also established the towns of Tarn Taran, Kartarpur, and Hargobinpura, and finished building Amritsar. Interestingly, the period of Guru Amar Das, Guru Ram Das, and Guru Arjun Dev coincides with the rule of Emperor Akbar over India, who was particularly impressed by the teachings of Sikh Gurus and by Sikh institutions. The people of the Punjab enjoyed a relatively peaceful life under the Mughal rulers, who had a major impact on the development of Sikh tradition. During this period, the number of Sikhs increased by many times and trade flourished in the four towns Guru Arjun Dev built.

The death of Emperor Akbar brought on a sudden reversal in the policy of the state toward the Sikhs. The new emperor, Jehangir, disapproved of the growing popularity of Guru Arjun and he ordered his arrest on the charge that he helped Jehangir's son, Prince Khusrau, in a rebellion. Guru Arjun was arrested and removed to Lahore, where he was executed on May 30, 1606. Guru Arjun is remembered, with profound grief, as the first martyr in the Sikh tradition.

Guru Hargobind (1595–1644)

The death of Guru Arjun was a turning point in the history of the Punjab. His son Hargobind took over the leadership of the Sikh community in 1606. At his investiture, he wore two swords: one to symbolize *piri* (spiritual power); the other *miri* (temporal authority). The term *mir* means chieftain/king and *piri* denotes spiritual guide/leader, both terms coming from Muslim culture. Under his leadership, the Sikh movement entered a new phase that gave birth to the new policy of defending one's faith. Guru Hargobind issued *hukamnamas* (orders) to Sikhs to offer horses and arms as *daswandh* (literally, donating a tenth of one's earnings to the Guru).

Guru Hargobind built the *Akal Takhat* in 1609 facing the Golden Temple. The name *Akal Takhat* is composed of two words: *Akal*, meaning the Timeless God, and *Takhat*, denoting a throne (thus the throne of the Timeless God). The *Akal Takhat* was reserved for discussing social and political matters concerning Sikhs, while the Golden Temple represented the spiritual authority. Its establishment signified a turning point in the development of Sikh tradition. Guru Hargobind trained his followers in martial arts and they fought battles with the Mughal authorities. Once he was imprisoned in the fort of Gawalior, but soon after his release, Guru Hargobind shifted his headquarters to Kiratpur, a town he established in the foothills of the Himalayas, where he died in 1644.

Guru Har Rai (1630–1661)

Before his death in 1644, Guru Hargobind appointed his grandson Har Rai—whose absence from the main centers of the Sikh movement, within the Punjab, seriously affected the spread of Sikhism—as successor. Guru Har Rai's seventeen years of leadership were not marked by any noteworthy events.

Guru Hari Krishan (1656–1664)

Guru Hari Krishan was only five years old when appointed to the guruship. Moreover, Mughal Emperor Aurangzeb exploited internal divisions within the Guru's household and appointed himself to arbitrate the conflicting claims between Guru Hari Krishan and his elder brother, Ram Rai. While in Delhi, Guru Hari Krishan was stricken with smallpox and died. According to Sikh tradition, Guru Hari Krishan uttered *Baba Bakaley* (literally, grandfather is at Bakala) before dying. His declaration created serious problems in finding a successor.

Guru Teg Bahadur (1621–1675)

Guru Teg Bahadur had been living in Bakala since the death of his father, Guru Hargobind. Teg Bahadur was the son of Nanaki, Guru Hargobind's second of three wives. After the death of the eighth Guru, Hari Krishan, twenty-two claimants to the *guruship* set up headquarters in Bakala. According to Sikh tradition, one devoted Sikh named Makhan Shah Lubana resolved the issue by testing the credentials of the self-appointed gurus. He eventually succeeded in finding the true guru, Teg Bahadur.

Guru Teg Bahadur established his headquarters at Anandpur and went on an extensive tour of India to meet the Sikh *sangats*. He was accompanied by his wife Gujri, who gave birth to their son Gobind Rai at Patna, where the Sikhs erected a magnificent *gurdwara*, now regarded as one of the five *takhats* (thrones) of the Sikhs.

Guru Gobind Singh (1666–1708)

The tenth Guru, Gobind Singh, was only nine years old when he assumed leadership after the execution of his father, who was publicly beheaded in Delhi in 1675. At that time, the tenth Guru's name was Gobind Rai. In his autobiography *Apni Katha* (my story), the tenth Guru wrote, "I came into this world charged with the duty to uphold the right in every place; to destroy sin and evil. O you holy men, know it well in your hearts that the only reason I took birth was to see that righteousness may flourish; that the good may live and tyrants be torn out by their roots." Like his grandfather Hargobind, he welcomed arms and horses as *daswandh* and also invited able-bodied young men to join his mission. Gobind Rai fought many battles with local

Hindu rulers and prepared his followers for the major tasks that lay ahead.

THE FOUNDING OF THE KHALSA

The term *Khalsa* is applied to the community of initiated Sikhs established by the tenth Guru, Gobind Singh, at Anandpur in 1699. *Khalsa* is derived from the Arabic *khalis*, meaning pure or unadulterated; it also refers to land under direct control of the crown. Both these meanings provide deep insight into the strategic planning of Guru Gobind Singh in establishing the institution of the *Khalsa*. At the time, he was engaged in eliminating internal divisions within the Sikh movement by creating a central authority under his direct control. He was also confronted by the repressive policies of the Mughal government, which was determined to eliminate the Sikh movement once and for all.

Tradition focuses on two main factors that were crucial to the founding of the *Khalsa*. The first is directly related to the death and manner of execution of the ninth Guru, Teg Bahadur. The second factor was the cowardly behavior of those Sikhs who were present at the time of the execution and did not come forward to collect the Guru's torso and severed head. Instead, they drew back to avoid recognition for fear of persecution; for at that time one could not distinguish a Sikh from his appearance alone.

Another major challenge came from the *masands* (Guru's nominated officials), who had become the main source of internal strife within the Sikh movement. Many *masands* had established themselves as gurus and refused to acknowledge the authority of Gobind Singh.

According to tradition, the tenth Guru invited his followers from all over the country to gather at Anandpur on the occasion of the festival of *Baisakhi*. After the morning service, the Guru appeared before the huge congregation, drew his sword from its scabbard, and demanded five men for sacrifice. It is said that the congregation was stunned to hear this demand. After a few moments, one Sikh rose to offer himself. He was taken into the tent by the Guru, who reappeared with his sword dripping with blood and asked for another for sacrifice. In this manner, five men were taken into the tent to be sacrificed. Then, to everybody's amazement, the Guru came out of the tent with the five volunteers, who were wearing saffron-colored clothes like those of the Guru. At that moment, the Guru declared that the *panj pyarey* (five beloved ones) were to be the nucleus of a new and dynamic community called the *Khalsa*.

After selection of the *panj pyarey*, Gobind Singh created an innovative initiation ceremony called the *amrit*, which literally means water of immortality (used in the Sikh initiation ceremony); it is also known as *khandey di pahul* (water of the double-edged sword). Thus, the tenth Guru discarded the centuries-old tradition of *charan pahul*. Before the founding of the *Khalsa*, the initiation ceremony was conducted with water touched by a guru's toe, thus the term *charan pahul* (*charan* means foot, *pahul* denotes water).

The new-style initiation ceremony was fundamentally different from the traditional mode of initiation. Preparation of the *amrit* was one of the defining factors of the new rite. First, the Guru poured water into a steel bowl and stirred it with a double-edged sword while reciting hymns from the Adi Granth, including some of his own compositions. It is said that the Guru's wife added some sugar into the bowl during preparation of the *amrit*. Then the Guru offered *amrit* to the *panj pyarey*, who, most importantly, belonged to different caste groups. They drank the *amrit* from the same bowl, signifying their entry into the casteless fraternity of the *Khalsa*. The *panj pyarey* then took the following vows:

1) My father is the tenth Guru, Gobind Singh.

2) My mother is Mata Sahib Devan (wife of Guru Gobind Singh).

3) My place of birth is Anandpur.

These vows further reinforced the notion of a corporate *Khalsa* brotherhood.

After the initiation ceremony, the next most significant innovation was the change in the names of the *panj pyarey*. All five volunteers, like the Guru, had traditional Hindu/Indic names before their initiation. They were then given a new corporate name: *Singh*. It is significant to examine the meaning of the title *Singh*. The word is derived from the Sanskrit *simbha*, meaning lion; it had been in common use by Hindu princes as a surname. Thus, the tenth Guru elevated the status of ordinary people to that of the *Kashatriyas* (warrior and princely caste group).

The climax of the initiation ceremony occurred when the Guru received *amrit* from the *panj pyarey* and changed his name from Gobind Rai to Gobind Singh. It is of note that Guru Gobind Singh admitted women into the *Khalsa*. After the initiation, a woman receives the title of *Kaur*, which means princess (for example, Kiran Kumari would become Kiran Kaur after the initiation ceremony).

Let us look at the names of the *panj pyarey* before and after the initiation rite:

BEFORE INITIATION	AFTER INITIATION
1) Daya Ram	1) Daya Singh
2) Dharam Das	2) Dharam Singh
3) Mohkam Chand	3) Mohkam Singh
4) Sahib Chand	4) Sahib Singh
5) Himat Rai	5) Himat Singh

The *amrit* ceremony initiated the concept of a distinctive corporate identity within the Sikh movement. It also removed the fear of death from the minds of new initiates. By admitting women into the *Khalsa* brotherhood, it also reinforced the Sikh belief in the equality of humankind. It also deprived the *masands* of the privilege of conducting initiation rites and established the authority of the institution of the *panj pyarey* as representatives of the Guru. Since then, the *amrit* ceremony can be conducted only by five *amritdhari* (initiated) Sikhs, symbolizing the institution of the *panj pyarey* (five beloved ones).

According to tradition, Guru Gobind Singh also prescribed a new code of discipline for the members of the *Khalsa*, which includes the wearing of the five emblems, previously mentioned on page 5 and collectively known as *panj kakaar* (the Five Ks): kes, kargha, kirpan, kachha/kachhahira, and kara.

Since the names of Sikh emblems begin with the letter *kakka* in the *Gurmukhi* script, they are collectively known as the five *kakkey*. The letter *kakka* corresponds to the letter "K" of the Roman alphabet and thus the "Five Ks."

Finally, the guru prescribed four rules of conduct for members of the *Khalsa*. They must not cut their hair and must not smoke tobacco or consume alcohol. They should not eat *halal* (meat slaughtered according to Muslim custom) but only *jhatka* meat, where the animal is slaughtered with one blow. Finally, they must not molest women in general and Muslim ladies in particular. As mentioned on page 6, a detailed and comprehensive code of discipline (Rahit Maryada) was approved by the Shiromani Gurdwara Parbandhak Committee.

It is important to note that a turban is not one of the prescribed emblems but has far greater significance for Sikhs than any other head-covering, as it is worn to control *kes* (one of the Five Ks). A male Sikh is required to wear a turban in public, which is regarded as a symbol of honor.

The founding of the *Khalsa* alarmed local Hindu princes, who with the support of the Mughal army forced Guru Gobind to evacuate Anandpur. He moved to Deccan and established his headquarters at Nanded, where he learned about the death of Emperor Aurangzeb. Gobind Singh was fully conversant with the political climate of the Punjab. He dispatched Banda, one of his trusted disciples, to lead the Punjabi Sikhs, and in 1710 Banda established the first sovereign Punjabi/Sikh state. By the time he was captured in 1716, he had inspired the Punjabi people to determine their own destiny.

As a result of Banda's miraculous achievement, in 1799, Maharaja Ranjit Singh, leader of one of the Sikh *misls* (armies), captured Lahore and laid the foundation for an independent Punjabi/Sikh state in the Punjab. Ranjit Singh disbanded the Sikh *misls* and emerged as sovereign ruler of the Punjab, where he died in 1839. Within ten years of his death, the Punjab was taken over by the British in 1849.

3

Scriptures

Without the Guru there is no divine knowledge,
without faith no meditation;
Without truth there is no credit,
and without capital no balance.

—Guru Nanak

ADI GRANTH

The principal scripture of the Sikh community is called the Adi Granth. It was compiled by the fifth Guru, Arjun Dev, who completed this work in 1604. It is of note that 2004 is the four hundredth anniversary of this unique collection. The process of evolution and development of the Adi Granth is closely linked with the emergence and maturity of the Sikh tradition. The name Adi Granth provides deep insight into the central teachings of Sikhism, especially the concept of the oneness of God. The word *Adi* is derived from the Sanskrit for "original" or "eternal," and the term *Granth* denotes a book or a collection of compositions in book form.

The word *Adi* is found in Guru Nanak's most celebrated hymn *Japji*, which begins with the statement in the *Mul mantra* (basic creed) that God is *Adi Sach* (true from the beginning). Thus the title Adi Granth confirms the belief that Sikh scripture had its origins in eternity. The notion of eternity refers to the compositions in the Adi Granth, collectively known as *bani*.

Let us examine some of the terms applied by Sikh gurus that capture the meaning of the writings/compositions in the scriptures: *bani* (utterance), *gurbani* (Guru's utterance or spoken word), *dhur ki bani* (utterance from the beginning or eternity). The phrase *dhur ki bani* refers to the transcendental origin of the hymns contained in the Adi Granth. Reflecting on the nature of *dhur ki bani*, Guru Arjun wrote, "... *gurbani* has emanated from the Primal One, which has dispelled all my worries."

Addressing *Bhai* Lalo (a carpenter with whom he often stayed with at Aimnabad), Guru Nanak reflects on the revealed nature of the gurbani:

"Whatever Word I receive from the Lord,
I pass it on in the same strain, O, Lalo" [5]

Thus the Adi Granth contains the "Word of God," and Guru Nanak was the medium of God's message. Guru Nanak frequently regarded himself as a *dhadi* (minstrel) of God who proclaimed the glory of the divine word. He repeatedly asserted that his sayings were the result of direct communication from

God: "I speak only when you inspire me to speak, O Lord." [6] Expanding on the true nature of *bani*, Guru Amar Das said, "The *gurbani* is God himself and it is through it that man obtains union with God." [7] The fourth guru, Ram Das, said, "The *gurbani* is the Lord's name and this name I enshrine in my mind." [8] The compiler of the Adi Granth, Guru Arjun, proclaimed, "The holy book is the abode of God." [9]

To gain further understanding of the nature of *gurbani*, we begin by looking at the process of compiling the Adi Granth and the way it was transformed from Adi Granth to the Guru Granth Sahib, which, in fact, signifies the role of the institution of guruship in Sikh tradition.

The origin of the Adi Granth can be traced to Guru Nanak's first utterance—"There is no Hindu and there is no Muslim"— and his first composition, which is popularly known as the *Mul-Mantra*. The opening phrase, *Ek Onkar*, of the *Mul-Mantra* summarizes the fundamental belief of Sikhism. The word *Ek* means one and *Onkar* denotes God, thus the first emphasis is on the oneness of God. The Adi Granth begins with the *Mul-Mantra*, which occurs more than one hundred times throughout the text. It signifies the centrality of the belief in the concept of the oneness of God in Sikhism.

Compilation of the Adi Granth began during the period of Guru Nanak's travels. Alongside his own compositions, Guru Nanak collected and recorded the writings of Muslim and Hindu saints in a book called a *pothi* (volume). It is important to note that Hindu and Muslim contributors to the Adi Granth composed their songs over a period of six centuries before Guru Nanak's arrival. Before his death, Guru Nanak made the most important decision of appointing his successor, Angad Dev, and handed over his *pothi*/notebook to Guru Angad Dev. Thus, Guru Nanak Dev laid the basis of the new tradition in which the positions of the Guru and the disciple were interchangeable: they represented one and the same light.

During the last fifteen years of his life at Kartarpur, Guru Nanak attracted a significant number of followers. Like Guru

Nanak, his successor Guru Angad Dev also composed *bani* that he included in Guru Nanak's *pothi*. He had prepared a number of copies of the collection for use by his disciples in other places. Before his death, Guru Angad Dev handed over Guru Nanak's notebook along with his own writings to his successor, Guru Amar Das.

By this time, the Sikh movement had spread to many towns and villages throughout the Punjab. In order to cater to the growing demands of the Sikh, Guru Amar Das introduced the system of *manjis* (seat of authority) and appointed his representatives to organize worship and collection of offerings. He had made more copies of the *bani* of his predecessors and included his own compositions. Reflecting on the nature of the compositions, Guru Amar Das wrote, "The *gurbani* is God himself and it is through *gurbani* that man obtains union with God." [10] Thus, Guru Amar Das further reinforced the concept that *gurbani* had the ultimate authority.

Before his death, Guru Amar Das appointed Ram Das—who happened to be his son-in-law—as his successor. Guru Ram Das shifted his headquarters to Ramdaspur, which later became Amritsar. Following the tradition of his predecessors, Guru Ram Das also composed *bani*. Most importantly, he nominated his youngest son, Arjun Dev, as his successor. Guru Arjun Dev also composed *bani*. It was Guru Arjun Dev who took the historic step to bring together all the writings into a single volume for the benefit of the entire Sikh community. The whole collection was meticulously edited by Guru Arjun Dev and was given the most revered title of Adi Granth. The last verse of the scriptures is called *Mandavani*, meaning a seal in which Guru Arjun Dev reflects on the significance of the final volume. It reads:

> In this plate are placed three things: truth, contentment, and meditation. The nectar-name of the Lord, the support of all, has also been put therein. If someone eats this food, if someone relishes it, he is emancipated ...[11]

Interestingly, compilation of the Adi Granth and construction of the *Harimandir* (Golden Temple) began simultaneously and both were completed in 1604. Guru Arjun Dev installed the Adi Granth in the Golden Temple and appointed Bhai Buddha, a Jat (peasant caste) Sikh, as the first *granthi* (official reader and custodian of the Adi Granth). His appointment introduced a new and dynamic factor in the traditional culture of Punjabi society, as it challenged the role of Brahmins, who for centuries had control over the teaching and learning of Hindu scriptures.

The original copy of the Adi Granth is popularly known as *Kartarpur wali Bir* (literally, Adi Granth of Kartarpur). It remained with the descendants of Guru Arjun Dev until the founding of Sikh rule in the Punjab in 1799. Soon after, the Adi Granth was removed to the court of Maharaja Ranjit Singh in Lahore. In 1849, when the British captured Lahore, Sodhi Sadhu Singh, a descendant of the Sikh gurus, petitioned the British authorities for its return. He prepared a copy of the Adi Granth, which he presented to Queen Victoria as a token of gratitude. This volume is now in the Record Office of the India Library in London.

Since then, the original copy of the Adi Granth has remained in the possession of the Sodhi family at Kartarpur. On major festivals, it is ceremonially displayed so that Sikh pilgrims can have a *darshan* (glimpse) and make generous offerings to the scriptures.

From the Adi Granth to Guru Granth Sahib

The transition from human guruship to that of the guruship invested in the Adi Granth was a slow process. The period after the martyrdom of Guru Arjun Dev in 1606 and that of ninth Guru Teg Bahadur created a situation of uncertainty and confusion in the Sikh community. There were internal problems concerning the guruship within the guru household that confronted the tenth Guru, Gobind Singh.

According to Sikh tradition, Gobind Singh prepared the final version of the Adi Granth by adding the *bani* of his father, ninth

Guru Teg Bahadur. It was completed in 1706 at a place called Dam Dama Sahib. Thus, the final version of the Adi Granth is known as the *Dam Dama Vali Bir*, and it is regarded as the authorized version.

Tradition records that before his death in 1708, tenth Guru Gobind Singh terminated the line of human gurus by bestowing guruship on the Adi Granth. The ceremony of the transfer of personal authority to the scripture is believed to have taken place at Nanded in Maharashtra state. Since that moment, the Adi Granth has been revered as a human guru and is addressed as the Guru Granth Sahib.

The term *Sahib* is from Islamic tradition and means lord. This signifies the highest authority accorded to the Adi Granth by the Sikhs. It is important to note that the Adi Granth is always positioned at a higher level than the congregation, who sit on the floor. The presence of the Adi Granth is mandatory at important religious ceremonies. Before the culmination of a service, it is opened by the *granthi* at random, and the first hymn on the left-hand page is read out to the *sangat*; this reading is called the *hukamnama* (guru's order for the day), and it signifies culmination of the service, with the authority of the guru as personified by the Adi Granth.

The centrality of the Adi Granth can be understood by observing the way Sikhs show their reverence during services. A Sikh would approach the Adi Granth with folded hands and then bow by touching the floor with his forehead, leaving offerings before the scripture. A Sikh attendant waves a *chauri* (ritual fan) over the scripture during the service, which is symbolic of the highest authority of the Adi Granth. At night the scripture is ceremonially wrapped in *rumalas* (a large piece of expensive material usually donated by Sikh families) and then taken to the resting room called the *sach khand* (sacred dwelling), located on the top floor of the gurdwara. The scripture is always carried on the head when transported from one place to another, which signifies its authority and the reverence expressed by Sikhs.

However, all Sikhs do not believe in termination of the human guruship by Guru Gobind Singh. The Namdhari Sikhs, for example, believe in the continuity of the line of human gurus, although they have a very high regard for the Guru Granth Sahib (Adi Granth).

Language of the Adi Granth

The Adi Granth is written in *Gurmukhi* (from the guru's mouth) script. Creation of the *Gurmukhi* script is attributed to the second Guru, Angad Dev. But there is diversity of opinion about the origin and antiquity of the Punjabi language and *Gurmukhi* script. It is generally accepted that the language of the Adi Granth is Punjabi; however, the language of the largest portion of the scriptures is Sant Bhasha or Hindvi, which is the mixture of Hindi, Prakrit, Braj, and Punjabi.

The current volume of the Adi Granth has 1,430 pages. It contains 5,894 hymns (*shabads* and *shalokas*). The total number of hymns attributed to each contributor is as follows: [12]

Guru Nanak Dev	974
Guru Angad Dev	62
Guru Amar Das	907
Guru Ram Das	679
Guru Arjun Dev	2,218
Guru Teg Bahadur	116

The Hindu and Muslim contributors, popularly called *bhagats*, include the following: [13]

Kabir	541
Farid	116
Namdev	60
Ravidas	41
Satta and Balwand	8
Sunder	6
Trilochan	4
Beni	3
Dhanna	3
Mardana	3
Jai Dev	2
Bhikhan	2
Sadna	1
Ramanand	1
Pipa	1
Sain	1
Parmanand	1
Surdas	1

Another feature of the Adi Granth is its arrangement according to a musical setting called *ragas*, in which each hymn is meant to be sung. For example, at the Golden Temple, a relay of religious musicians (*ragis*) continuously perform *shabad-kirtan* strictly according to the prescribed setting by fifth Guru Arjun Dev. It was the first Guru, Nanak Dev, who introduced the tradition of devotional singing that has emerged as an integral part of the Sikh service everywhere.

Dasam Granth

The second scripture of the Sikhs is popularly known as the *Dasam Granth*, meaning the *Granth* of tenth Guru Gobind Singh. Guru Gobind Singh was a great poet, believed to have composed poetry on many topics and in many languages. He had fifty-two poets and scholars in his court at Anandpur. According to Sikh tradition, most of the Guru's writings and the works of other poets were lost during the time of the abandonment of Anandpur under severe pressure from the Mughal army. After the death of Guru Gobind Singh in 1708, Mani Singh, one of the Guru's trusted disciples, collected the writings of Guru Gobind Singh, a task completed in 1734 at Amritsar.

For a considerable time during the late eighteenth and early nineteenth centuries, both scriptures were installed side by side on the same platform and received the same reverence. However, with the rise of the Singh Sabha Reform movement, the Dasam Granth was relegated to a lower status. In 1885, the Singh Sabha appointed a committee of scholars to resolve the problematic issue of the scripture's authenticity. In 1902, the committee published an authorized version of the scripture, which was finally given the title of Dasam Granth. This version is now in general circulation and is 1,428 pages in length.

It is important to note that the Dasam Granth receives equal reverence at the historical gurdwaras of Nanded and Patna Sahib, where it is installed alongside the Adi Granth. At the culmination of the service, both scriptures are ritually opened for the *hukamnamas*, which are read to the *sangat* and also recorded on a blackboard for those who are not present at the service. In fact, both scriptures used to be present at meetings of the *Sarbat Khalsa* (literally, gathering of all members of the Khalsa) and both received the same reverence.

Although the Dasam Granth is written in *Gurmukhi* script, the language of most hymns is Braj, which is a mixture of Sanskrit and Hindi. Two compositions are in Persian, one of which is called Zafar Mama, a long letter to the Mughal emperor Aurangzeb by tenth Guru Gobind Singh.

Another long composition is called *Bachitar Natak* (wonderful drama). It is believed to be the autobiography of Guru Gobind Singh. The Dasam Granth also contains several hymns that are recited at the *Baisakhi* festival and also at the birth anniversary of tenth Guru Gobind Singh. Although the *Dasam Granth* is not installed in the gurdwaras, some of its compositions are recited during preparation of the *amrit* (water prepared for the initiation ceremony) and other acts of worship.

The Compositions of Bhai Gurdas

Bhai Gurdas occupies an important position within the Sikh tradition. He was the scribe who wrote out the Adi Granth under the direction of Guru Arjun Dev. Collections of his writings are popularly known as *varan* (ballads), which are regarded as "the key" to the Adi Granth and are normally sung by Sikh musicians at the gurdwaras.

4

Worldview

All are created from the seed of God.
There is the same clay in the whole world,
the potter (God) makes many kinds of pots.

—Guru Amar Das, Bhairo

Sikhism is a world-oriented tradition. Sikhs perceive the world as *dharmsal* (the abode of God). The central teaching in Sikhism is the oneness of God, which is expressed in the phrase *Ek Onkar*, meaning: "There is but one God." The symbol of Ek Onkar is often found adorned on *gurdwaras* (places of worship). All people, irrespective of caste, creed, color, and gender, are regarded as the creation of one God. In order to comprehend the deep meanings inherent in the doctrine of the oneness of God, we must look at the historical context in which Guru Nanak enunciated and developed the message of universal love and divine truth. Interaction between the Hindu and Muslim traditions was one of the unique features for the basis of universalism in the teachings of Guru Nanak, which he declared in his pronouncement that "there is no Hindu and there is no Muslim." This declaration clearly emphasizes the unity and equality of humankind. In fact, Guru Nanak was inviting people to engage themselves in the search for the "divine" reality that lay beyond sectarian boundaries.

ONE HUMAN FAMILY
The multifaith environment in which the Sikh tradition emerged and developed provided unique opportunities for understanding the true meaning of belonging to one human family. This pluralistic environment endowed the Sikh community with tolerance and a desire to learn from other religious traditions. It also generated a new climate for translating the message of diversity in God's kingdom into reality, and resulted in the creation of some unique Sikh institutions. For example, the Adi Granth is living testimony of such a unique divine experience: Alongside the compositions of the Sikh Gurus, the Adi Granth contains the writings of Muslim and Hindu saints, some of whom belonged to the lowest strata of Hindu society. Thus, the Adi Granth not only represents the combined wisdom of a multifaith society but also imparts a message of the unity and equality of humankind.

DIVERSITY: A DYNAMIC AND POSITIVE FORCE

The teachings and the structure of Sikh scripture made an important contribution to an increasing understanding that human beings are the creation of one eternal reality called God. Another manifestation of the notion of the oneness of God is the architecture of the Golden Temple: its four doors symbolize the omnipresence of God. Both the Adi Granth and the Golden Temple uniquely represent a most enriching experience in the history of humankind, in which the concept of diversity in God's kingdom has been celebrated as a key factor for shaping future human relations.

GURU NANAK DEV'S DIVINE EXPERIENCE

I was a minstrel out of work

The Lord gave we employment,

The mighty One instructed me,

"Night and day, sing my praise."

The Lord summoned the minstrel

to His High Court,

On me He bestowed the robe of

honouring Him and singing His praise,

On me He bestowed the Nectar in a cup,

the Nectar of His True and Holy name.

Those who at the bidding of the Guru

feast and take their fill of the

Lord's holiness attain peace and joy.

Your minstrel spreads your glory

by singing Your Word.

Nanak, through adoring the truth

We attain to the All-highest.*

* Adi Granth, 150.

In Sikhism, the diversity of God's kingdom is perceived as a dynamic and positive force. It is believed that all religious traditions are equally valid and capable of enlightening their followers. Sikhism rejects the view that any particular religious tradition has a monopoly regarding "Absolute Truth." Sikhism strongly rejects the practice of converting people to other religious traditions. It is believed that truly following the teachings of one's faith makes a person *gurmukh* (guru-orientated). Guru Nanak said, "God is everywhere. He has created us all. He who realizes this is a true Hindu or a Muslim." This equality is further emphasized by the statement that "Although there are two paths, the Hindu and the Muslim but ... there is only one God."

GOD

In the Sikh teachings, God is conceived as being without form or shape (*nirankar*). Therefore no image or idol can represent God. The multilingual nature of Indian society made a valuable contribution toward the development of universalism in Sikhism. Linguistic diversity was an important tool in the hands of the Sikh Gurus, who employed it most creatively to transmit the message of the oneness of God. In Sikhism, God has been identified by many different names, which originated in various religious and linguistic traditions: Allah, Khuda, Kadar, and Karim are from Muslim and Arabic traditions; Brahm, Parmatma, Bhagwan, Ishwar, and Hari derive from Hindu and Sanskrit traditions. These names occur again and again in the compositions of the Sikh Gurus and other contributors to Sikh scripture. It is important to note that the central *gurdwara* of the Sikhs is called *Harimandir* (Golden temple). According to Sikh teachings, all human groups evolved and developed their modes of worship and religious traditions within the context of their social milieu. While a Muslim prayer is called a *namaz*, for a Hindu it is a *puja*, and a Sikh prayer is called an *ardas* or *path-karna*. The tenth Guru, Gobind Singh, highlighted the essence and universality of religious truth as follows:

Recognize all mankind, whether Muslim or Hindu as one.
The same God is the Creator and Nourisher of all;
Recognize no distinctions among them.
The temple and mosque are the same;
So are the Hindu worship and Muslim prayer.
Human beings are all one.[14]

It is significant to note that at the culmination of their service, Sikhs all over the world pray for the well-being and prosperity of the whole of humankind.

MONOTHEISM

Guru Nanak and his successor Gurus were strict monotheists. They preached the notion of the oneness of God and the whole world as His/Her creation. They disapproved of the worship of idols and a belief in the reincarnation of God. It is believed that God is without form, color, mark, or lineage, and therefore cannot be installed or established as an idol. In Sikhism, God is perceived as infinite and *ajuni* (beyond birth and death), thus He/She cannot die to be reincarnated, or assume human form as Hindus believe and worship Lord Rama and Krishna as God who appeared in human form on Earth.

SOCIAL JUSTICE

The concept of social justice stems from Guru Nanak's declaration in which he describes Earth as a *dharmsal* established by God within the universe. The term *dharmsal* is made up of two words: *dharm*, which means religious, moral, and social obligations, and *sal*, which denotes a place of abode. It is also believed that the earth and everything that stands on it carries the divine stamp. In Sikhism, the world is perceived as the abode of God and a place to practice *dharma*, which means that all human beings should engage themselves in righteous actions and behavior in order to create a just social order. Sikhism is a living tradition, and a Sikh is expected to demonstrate his/her *dharma* through social responsibility. A

Sikh is not a passive spectator in this world but an active participant in the drama of human affairs. Thus for a Sikh, there is no place for renunciation of society, celibacy, or pursuit of God in the forest. Guru Nanak denounced the *Yogis* who preached and practiced renunciation of society and praised those who faced the challenge of their social responsibilities. For a Sikh, a life of truthful conduct is more important than a simple vision of truth alone. Sikhs must therefore work hard and earn their living, and must not depend on other people like a parasite.

In Sikhism, the concept of *kirat karna* signifies one of the cardinal rules of social and ethical behavior. *Kirat* literally means work and *karna* denotes "to do." The principle of *kirat karna* has greatly contributed to forging social awareness among the Sikhs. Guru Nanak said that those who depend on the earnings of others and exploit them for their own selfish gratification lead a worthless life. He also declared that "Encroachment upon what rightfully belongs to others is forbidden to both Muslims and Hindus, as pork to the former and beef to the latter." [15]

Sikhs learn about the significance of the notion of *kirat karna* by remembering the historic episode of Bhai Lalo and Malik

CONDEMNATION OF RELIGIOUS HYPOCRISY

Guru Nanak condemned religious hypocrisy of Yogis (mendicants) and their renunciation of social obligations:

> Let contentment be your yogi earnings;
> Let modesty be your pouch and begging bowl;
> Let meditation be the ashes you religiously wear;
> Let consciousness of death be your head-covering;
> Let pure living be your vow of celibacy
> And faith in God your staff.
> Accept all humans as your equals
> And let them be your only sect.[*]

* Adi Granth, 6.

Bhago. According to Sikh tradition, Guru Nanak stayed with Bhai Lalo at Aimnabad during his travels. Bhai Lalo was a carpenter who belonged to the low caste of *Shudras*. Malik Bhago, the landlord of the village, and other high-caste people disapproved of the choice of residence by Guru Nanak. One day Guru Nanak refused an invitation to a meal offered by Malik Bhago. It is said that Guru Nanak asked Malik Bhago to bring some food from his house; he also sent Bhai Lalo to fetch some of his food. Thereupon, Guru Nanak held Malik Bhago's piece of bread in his left hand and Bhai Lalo's bread in his right hand. Lifting his arms, Guru Nanak pressed the two pieces. It is believed that drops of milk came out of Bhai Lalo's bread, while Malik Bhago's bread was dripping with blood. Guru Nanak told Malik Bhago that his food was obtained by exploiting others, while the food of Bhai Lalo had been earned by honest labor.

Guru Nanak not only emphasized the principle of *kirat karna* but also introduced the concept of *wand chhakna*. The term *wand* means sharing, while *chhakna* denotes eating. The phrase *wand chhakna*, like *kirat karna*, signifies another important rule of Sikh behavior that has contributed enormously to generating social awareness among Sikhs. Guru Nanak preached the principles of *kirat karna* and *wand chhakna* for the social, moral, and spiritual development of his followers. The Sikh tradition of a communal meal (*langar*) at the gurdwaras is the manifestation of Guru Nanak's teachings. Guru Nanak said, "Only he who earns his living by the sweat of his brow and shares his earnings with others has discovered the path of righteousness."

The tradition of *daswandh* has contributed enormously to the development of Sikh tradition; it equipped the Sikh movement with financial resources and also helped to forge a special bond between a Sikh and his/her guru. It is important to note that all Sikh institutions are financially supported through regular donations made by Sikhs. A Sikh perceives the notion of *daswandh* as the most meritorious obligation; he/she regards their earnings as the Guru's grace. *Daswandh* is formed from two words: *das*, meaning ten, and *wandh*, denoting a share. It is generally accepted that the collection of *daswandh* was introduced by Guru Arjun Dev to raise funds for construction of the Golden Temple and other community projects. He instructed the *masands* (guru's appointees) to collect *daswandh* from Sikhs and bring it to Amritsar on the festival day of *Baisakhi*.

The collection of *daswandh* in its original form has become redundant. Nowadays, Sikhs make donations to a gurdwara on every visit. They also make generous donations to such historical gurdwaras as the Golden Temple. Most Sikh families make special donations to the historical *gurdwaras* at the time of a child's wedding. The establishment of *gurdwaras* during the Sikh diaspora has been financed by local Sikh communities, and such donations are regarded as *daswandh*. Interestingly, the tradition of *daswandh* is most popular among the Namdhari Sikhs, who passionately believe in the continuity of the line of living gurus. They regularly set aside a portion of their earnings as *daswandh* for their guru. Usually, the funds are sent to their guru's headquarters at Bhaini Sahib in the Punjab.

SEWA (VOLUNTARY SERVICE)

Sewa literally means voluntary/selfless service performed for the community. The institution of gurdwara plays an important role in promoting the ideal of human equality. Everyone— irrespective of caste, color, creed, or gender—is welcome to the gurdwara, and is offered *langar* (communal meal) and *karah- parshad* (blessed food) without distinction. Most Sikhs, particularly children, learn their initial lessons of *sewa* by helping in the community kitchen. Sikhs feel privileged to perform sewa at the *gurdwara*: They cook and serve food, clean utensils, and clean the kitchen and dining hall as part of their service.

Sikh children learn the fundamental principles of Sikh tradition at the gurdwaras. Their belief in the equality of human beings is confirmed as soon as they enter the congregational hall. They begin to appreciate the equality of sexes when their mothers and fathers sit on the same carpet in the gurdwara with other members of the congregation. They also see Sikh women reading the Adi Granth, as well as taking part in the *shabad-kirtan* (religious singing). Sikh women obtain inspiration from the teachings of the Sikh Gurus, who rejected the traditional view that women were inherently inferior.

Most parents encourage their children to perform *sewa* at the gurdwara. They serve food in the dining hall and sometimes look after the shoes of the *sangat*. Before every service, volunteers clean and prepare the main congregation hall. Until the mid-1970s, all religious functionaries at the gurdwaras in the United Kingdom were *sewadars* (volunteers). Selfless and voluntary service is one of the cardinal principles of Sikh conduct. The notion of *sewa* is closely linked with the concept of *dharmsal* espoused by Guru Nanak, who taught his followers to engage in righteous deeds by serving the community. Bhai Gurdas, scribe of the Adi Granth, emphasized the importance of *sewa* and sharing food as follows:

> The Sikhs should serve one another;
> Only by serving others, one can attain happiness;
> One should cultivate selfless devotion
> and share one's food with others.[16]

The establishment of gurdwaras is regarded as true *sewa* by Sikhs. The *kar sewa* (voluntary service for cleaning silt from the reservoir of the Golden Temple) is regarded as one of the most auspicious acts of *sewa*. The holy reservoir is cleaned at regular intervals and all Sikhs cherish this task. Many travel to Amritsar, while others send donations for this most momentous event.

Guru Nanak wrote extensively on the significance of voluntary service: "A place in God's court can only be attained if we do service to others in this world."[17] He was most critical of the conduct of contemporary leaders of various traditions and warned that "Wandering ascetics, warriors, celibates, *sannyasis* [renouncers of society], none of them obtains fruit [spiritual liberation] without performing *sewa*."[18] Evidently, the spirit of *sewa* played a key role in generating a new social and religious awareness among the Sikhs.

HUKAM (DIVINE ORDER)

The doctrine of *hukam* plays an important role in understanding the mystery of human existence within the universe. The term *hukam* came to Punjabi vocabulary from the Arabic tradition, and it means Divine Order. *Hukam* literally means command or order and *hakam* signifies the one who issues a command or order. The Sikh Gurus applied the concept of *hukam* extensively in their *bani* to elaborate the nature of creation, the universe, and human life. In Sikhism, it is believed that everything in the world functions according to a Divine Order or scheme. Guru Nanak, in his celebrated hymn called *Japji*, refers to the notion of *hukam* in order to emphasize the mysterious hand of God that is behind the functioning of the universe and the daily life of human beings.

Human life is regarded as the most precious divine gift and the highest form of existence in the universe. It is also perceived as part of the Divine Order, and it is therefore man's utmost obligation to submit to God's Will. Expanding on the true meaning of the concept of *hukam*, Sikh Gurus refer to the most significant aspects of human existence, such as birth and death, which are beyond man's control: the death of a person, whether she/he is young or old, is expressed as God's *hukam* and one must submit to His/Her Will.

Guru Nanak explained the notion of *hukam* by posing a question:

> How may man purify himself?
> How does man demolish the wall of ignorance?
> This is brought about by living in accordance with
> God's Command or Will. [19]

According to Sikh teachings, there is a Divine purpose in everything; a Sikh must thus have unquestionable faith in the concept of *hukam*. Sikh Gurus emphasize that human beings cannot know the Divine mysteries; they are only a drop in the ocean or like a tiny fish in the sea. It is therefore their *dharma* to submit before the Will of God. Sikh Gurus have emphatically reiterated in their teachings that in the end falsehood or evil will be destroyed and Divine Truth will prevail. For example, the martyrdom of the fifth Guru, Arjun Dev, as well as ninth Guru Teg Bahadur, is perceived as *hukam* to which they submitted without questioning.

Interestingly, the doctrine of *hukam* raises a fundamental question: Are human beings helpless creatures in this world? Sikh Gurus emphatically rejected this notion and taught that all human beings have been endowed with the facility to create their own destiny. If someone commits evil deeds, he/she will suffer accordingly. Moreover, it is abundantly clear that one reaps what one sows. Therefore, for the attainment of spiritual liberation one needs to engage him/herself in righteous deeds, which includes service to humanity.

AWAGAUN (CYCLE OF BIRTH AND DEATH)

Sikhs believe in the traditional Indic concept of *awagaun* (the cycle of birth and death). The concept of *awagaun* is based on the doctrine of *karma* (literally, actions or deeds) and transmigration of the soul. It is believed that there are 8,400,000 lives (*chaurasi lakh joon*) before one is reborn as a human being. The soul is regarded as immortal: it passes from one form of life to another depending upon one's deeds (*karma*) committed in life. Those who are sinful and engage in evil-doing keep circulating through the cycle of birth and death, which is regarded as the most degrading state.

In order to transcend the ultimate punishment of circulating through the cycle of birth and death, a Sikh is required to conduct him/herself according to the teachings of the Sikh Gurus. It is required that he/she must endeavor to become a *gurmukh* (guru-oriented), as opposed to a *manmukh* (self-oriented) person. Therefore, a Sikh must lead the life of an honest householder, a true believer in the oneness of God, while earning a living by honest means and sharing with others. At a Sikh funeral, the *granthi* recites the *antam-ardas* (last prayer) invoking God's forgiveness for the departed soul, thus saving him/her from the cycle of birth and death.

Sikhism rejects the traditional Indic view that one's low caste status is the result of bad conduct in a previous life. Sikhs strongly believe that human life is the most precious of all forms of life, and it is a divine gift. In this life, human beings have the choice to engage themselves in righteous deeds in order to transcend the bonds of birth and death and attain *mukti* (spiritual liberation). The true followers of a guru's teachings achieve the status of a *jiwan-mukta* (one who has conquered the worldly temptations and cut across the cycle of birth and death). The death of a *jiwan-mukta* is regarded as a gradual transition from earthly existence to an abode in heaven or the merging of one's soul with the Supreme Soul, called the *Parm-atma* (*Parm* means supreme, *atma* denotes soul or God).

5

Worship and
the Gurdwara

The stone he calls his god,
in the end, drowns him with itself
... Know that a boat of stone carries one not across.

—Guru Arjun Dev, Suhi

The essence of the notion of worship in Sikhism is remembrance of the "Nam" (God/Divine). The mode of Sikh worship falls into two main categories: individual and congregational. There are a number of terms applied to the act of Sikh worship, including *path karna, nam japna,* and *nam simran.*

Path karna literally means reciting a selection of hymns from the scripture. It can be undertaken anywhere that is quiet. One may also engage in the act of worship while performing domestic chores. Sikh women normally perform *path karna* in the morning while preparing food. Most Sikhs memorize the first five verses of Guru Nanak's hymn of *Japji* for individual worship, and many simply utter and repeat *waheyguru* (wonderful Lord, · meaning God). *Nam japna,* which means devoutly repeating the Divine Name/*waheyguru*, is another term popularly used for individual worship.

Most Sikh households keep a *gutka* (a small booklet containing a selection of hymns normally recited in daily worship). It is carefully wrapped in a clean cloth and kept in a safe place. Many devout Sikh families keep a copy of the Adi Granth in their homes; it is respectfully installed in a special room, usually located on a top floor. Technically, this location can be categorized as a *gurdwara*. In fact, it is a family *gurdwara* and as such not open to the general public. Members of the family respectfully call it *Babaji da kamra* (God's room).

Formalization of a uniform pattern of individual worship was finalized in 1945. It is prescribed in the *Rahit Maryada* (Sikh code of discipline) approved by the *Shiromani Gurdwara Parbandhak Committee* (Supreme Gurdwara Management Committee) in 1945 and published in 1951. Rules of daily worship called *nit-name* and personal cleanliness are prescribed for the guidance of the wider Sikh community. It comprises a selection of hymns from the scriptures:

A Sikh should rise early and take a bath, then recite the hymns of Japji, Jap, and Sawayyas.

At sunset he/she should recite the hymn of *Rahiras*.

Before going to bed he/she should recite the hymn of *Sohila*.

At the conclusion of each recital, the *ardas* (Sikh prayer) should be recited.

THE ROLE OF MODERN TECHNOLOGY

Today, most *gurdwaras* in the Punjab broadcast morning and evening prayers over loudspeakers. Recordings of *gurbani* from the Adi Granth and devotional music are available on audio cassettes and sold at most *gurdwaras*. Many Sikh families play audiotapes of devotional music early in the morning as the morning prayer. A number of local radio stations play tapes of *shabad-kirtan* during celebration of such Sikh festivals as *Baisakhi*. A few television channels specialize in broadcasting live recordings of morning *kirtan* from the *Harimandir Sahib* (Golden Temple). One TV station offered a live broadcast of the celebration for the four hundredth anniversary of the install-ment of the Adi Granth at the Golden Temple.

CONGREGATIONAL WORSHIP

The origin of congregational worship can be traced to Guru Nanak. According to Sikh tradition, after an extensive period of travels in India and abroad Guru Nanak settled at Kar-tarpur, where he laid down the foundation for the institution of the *gurdwara*. It was originally called a *dharmsala* (place of worship). Traditional *dharmsalas* in the Punjab were houses where travelers could spend the night. Kartarpur's *dharmsala* was distinctly unique: it became the focus for sharing and understanding the true meaning of the notion of the oneness of God. A congregation (*sangat*) of men and women from all caste groups would gather at the *dharmsala* to join in communal worship and *shabad-kirtan*. At the culmination of worship, members of the congregation would share a *langar* (communal meal). The institutions of *sangat*, *shabad-kirtan*, and *langar* emerged as the most distinguishing features of the Sikh tradition.

The Gurdwara

The *gurdwara* has emerged as one of the central institutions in the Sikh tradition. It has traditionally been a multipurpose institution. The *gurdwara* is the main center of congregational worship. It is also a place for social, spiritual, and moral nurturing, as well as a center for hospitality and service. The term *gurdwara* is composed of two words: *guru* and *dwara*. *Guru* literally means a teacher, a spiritual guide, and is also used for God, while *dwara* denotes "house" or "the doorway."

The origin of the term *gurdwara* is attributed to the sixth Guru, Hargobind, who is believed to have built *gurdwaras* on sites associated with his predecessors. Although *gurdwaras* differ in size and architectural design, they all have a copy of the Adi Granth. Another distinguishing feature of a *gurdwara* is the presence of a *nishan sahib* (Sikh flag), usually fixed near the building.

There are mainly two types of *gurdwaras*: historic and community-based. Historic *gurdwaras* are those buildings erected on sites that are important landmarks in the history of the Sikh movement: for example, Gurdwara Sis Ganj in Delhi, built on the spot where ninth Guru Teg Bahadur was publicly beheaded by Mughal authorities, and Gurdwara Kesgarh at Anandpur, where Guru Gobind Singh instituted the *Khalsa*.

There is no fixed day for holding congregational worship at a *gurdwara*, but in the diaspora most services take place on Sunday. There is a general pattern of Sikh service that is followed at all *gurdwaras*. It begins with the singing of Guru Nanak's hymn *Asa di var* in the morning, followed by more hymn singing from the Adi Granth. The service concludes with recitation of an *ardas* (Sikh prayer) by the *granthi* (reader of scripture), while members of the congregation stand silently with folded hands. After the *ardas*, a randomly chosen hymn from the scripture—called *hukamnama* (divine order for the day)—is read to the *sangat*. The service culminates in the distribution of *karah-parshad* (sanctified food) to all present, symbolizing the Sikh belief in the equality of humankind.

Attending a service at the *gurdwara* is regarded as most meritorious. Usually, all members of a Sikh family will go to the *gurdwara*, including the young children. Before entering the *gurdwara*, Sikhs bow toward the *nishan sahib* and touch the base of the mast as a symbol of respect and reverence. It is mandatory to remove shoes and cover heads before entering a congregational hall. A Sikh would then approach the palanquin under which the Adi Granth is placed on a *manji* (a small bed), and then bow and make an offering of money or food to be used in the kitchen. Men and women sit separately; this a Punjabi cultural tradition rather than Sikh belief.

During the service, men and women volunteers take part in the ritual of waving a *chauri* (ritual fan) over the scripture. Most Sikhs participate in preparation and distribution of the *langar*. Sikh parents encourage their children to do *sewa* at the *gurdwaras*.

The Nishan Sahib (The Sikh Flag)

The *nishan sahib* is one of the most distinguishable features of a *gurdwara*. It is a triangular flag with a Sikh emblem of a *Khanda*, comprising a double-edged sword fixed in a steel circle with two curved swords attached to a steel pole. The flag and the covering, reverentially called a *chola* (a long loose shirt worn by holy men), are made of saffron-colored material.

Every year the ceremony of *nishan sahib chardna* (replacing the old covering) takes place on the festival of *Baisakhi*, which usually falls on April 13. This ceremony begins with the recital of an *ardas*. The mast is lowered and the old covering is carefully removed. The mast is then ritually washed with a mixture of water and milk and dried with clean towels, and then a new covering is applied. Throughout this operation, members of the *sangat* and Sikh *sewadars* (volunteers) recite *shabads* (hymns). The mast with a new covering and flag is hoisted while a Sikh slogan is chanted: *Boley so nihal-sat sri akal* (anyone who utters the name of God is immortal and is a happy person). Normally, a new covering for the *nishan sahib* is donated by Sikh families.

Management Structure of the Gurdwaras

Historic *gurdwaras* are managed and controlled by a central body called the *Shiromani Gurdwara Parbandhak Committee* (Supreme Management Committee of Gurdwaras), which was constituted under the Punjab Gurdwara Act of 1925. Previously, all historic *gurdwaras* were under the control of *masands/ mahants* (appointees of Sikh gurus), who had become de facto owners of *gurdwara* property.

There is no tradition of priesthood in Sikhism. A *granthi* is an employee of the *gurdwara* management committee. He is appointed to read scripture and conduct other services. No formal qualifications are required for the post of a *granthi*. Although *granthis* are required to be trained, most of them learn *shabad-kirtan* from experienced *ragis* (musicians). The SGPC maintains a college for the training of *granthis* who are appointed to serve at historic *gurdwaras*. Generally, the position of a *granthi* is not regarded as high-status employment.

Community-Based Gurdwaras

There is a long tradition of building *gurdwaras* among the Sikhs, which is regarded as *sewa* (voluntary service). As soon as there is a reasonable number of Sikh residents in a town, they begin to establish a local *gurdwara*, which becomes the central place for celebrating religious festivals and other social functions. One of the distinguishable features of a community-based *gurdwara* is the nature of its management structure. These *gurdwaras* are managed and controlled by locally elected management committees that are answerable only to their *sangat*, and are completely autonomous institutions.

Another significant development within the Sikh movement is the emergence of caste-based *gurdwaras*, both in India and in the diaspora. Although Sikh Gurus vehemently rejected the notion of caste, it remains an important factor in the daily lives of Sikhs. Caste-based *gurdwaras* are one of the main instruments for perpetuating caste consciousness and caste solidarity. However, caste-based *gurdwaras*, like other *gurdwaras*, are open to all people irrespective of caste, creed, or gender. The fundamental difference lies in their management structure. For example, the membership of a Ramgarhia gurdwara is exclusively

HARIMANDIR SAHIB, THE GOLDEN TEMPLE

Harimandir Sahib is the central shrine of the Sikhs, the chief place of pilgrimage. The title *Harimandir Sahib* literally means the "Temple of God." The term *Hari* denotes God in Indic tradition, while *mandir* means "temple." The word *Sahib*, from the Arabic, is an honorific that means Lord or God.

The history of the land on which the *Harimandir*/Golden Temple stands is shrouded in mystery. Some traditions trace its origin back to the prehistoric times and hold that there was a reservoir of nectar (*amrit kund*) on the site. According to the Indic epic of the Ramayana, Sita, wife of Lord Rama, and their two sons stayed there during their exile. They fought a battle with their father, Lord Rama, in which he was wounded. However, when they learned the identity of their father, they brought some *amrit* (nectar) from the reservoir, which saved him, and some leftover nectar was poured into a nearby pond, which from that moment was transformed into a lake of nectar. There is one old tree in the *parkarma* (circumambulatory path around the reservoir) of the Golden Temple; it is reverentially called *Dukh, Bhanjni Beri* (remover of misery and illness), which is believed to stand on the same spot. Most Sikhs believe in the healing power of this tree.

It is also believed that Lord Buddha, along with some monks, passed by this site and proclaimed the place ideal for meditation. The Sikh tradition also claims that Guru Nanak visited this site during one of his missionary trips. Another local legend is associated with the episode of Rajani, daughter of Duni Chand, a revenue collector. It is claimed that her leprous husband was cured of his disease after a dip in the pond.

Sikh tradition records that the Mughal emperor Akbar once visited Goindwal, headquarters of third Guru Amar Das, but the Guru refused to meet him until he partook of *langar* in the Guru's kitchen. Akbar gladly accepted the Guru's invitation and was most impressed with the organization of the place, where everyone, irrespective of comprised of Ramgarhia Sikhs; every applicant for the membership is required to complete an application form and sign a declaration that reads, "I am a Ramgarhia Sikh."

caste, creed, and status, sat in rows and shared food. Before leaving Goindwal, Akbar donated a gift of land to Guru Amar Das, on which the whole complex of the Golden Temple stands today.

Let us look at some of the distinguishing features of the Golden Temple (which is pictured on page B of the photo insert). It has four doors, symbolizing the omnipresence of God. It is open to all people, irrespective of caste, creed, or gender. Furthermore, it rejects the view that facing any particular direction at the time of prayer has any significance for understanding the divine gift of belonging to the one human family.

The architecture of this structure represents both the Islamic and Indic traditions. For example, its domes reflect Muslim architecture, while its perpendicular pillars represent Indic tradition. In order to emphasize the notion of the oneness of God, fifth Guru Arjun Dev invited Mian Mir, a devout Muslim saint, to lay the foundation stone of the new temple. Most importantly, upon its completion, Guru Arjun Dev installed the first copy of the Adi Granth inside the Golden Temple.

The *Harimandir Sahib* stands in the middle of a rectangular reservoir called the *Amrit-Sarover* (a reservoir containing the water of immortality), which is surrounded by a *parkarma*. It can be approached via a causeway. The *Harimandir* got the name *Swarn Mandir* (Golden Temple) when its upper part was covered with gold-plated copper sheets during the reign of Maharaja Ranjit Singh in the early nineteenth century. The title *Golden Temple* was popularized by the British authorities in India.

Traditionally, most Sikh pilgrims take a ceremonial dip in the holy reservoir before entering the temple, which remains open throughout the day except for a short interval during the night (from midnight to 4:00 A.M.). During this period, the floor is washed with a mixture of milk and water by the *seawares* (volunteers) and is prepared to receive the Adi Granth, which is brought in during a procession from the *Akal Takhat*. A relay of religious musicians constantly sing hymns from the scripture for twenty-one hours each day.

Deras of Sants (Headquarters of Sikh Holy Men)

In Sikhism, a *Sant* is revered as a spiritual teacher/guide who is believed to be endowed with divine power. He is known by different titles, for example, *Sant, Baba Ji*, and *Guru Ji*. Sikhs operate from their headquarters, called *deras*. Their disciples show reverence by touching the *Sant*'s feet (the ritual of *matha tekna*) before seeking guidance concerning spiritual or domestic matters. *Sants* are also invited to bless their disciples on such auspicious occasions as weddings, the birth of a son, or opening of new businesses.

The authority of Sikh *Sants* stems from their claim to having been blessed by Guru Nanak's *darshan* (glimpse). In some ways a *Sant* acquires a reputation as a person who confers spiritual enlightenment and has healing power. Gradually, his residence becomes popular as a *dera*, and people normally wait for hours for a *darshan*. Some *Sants* regularly visit their disciples in the United Kingdom, Canada, and the United States. For example, Sant Charan Singh of Bhikhowal has a large following in England. A few years ago, he was invited by one of his followers, who had been blessed with the birth of a son. The family organized the ritual of *akhand-path* as instructed by Sant Charan Singh. After the end of the service, he addressed the *sangat*:

> I am an ordinary, uneducated person. Guru Nanak instructs me to spread his mission—my duty is to join you with the Guru Granth Sahib. Faith in Guru Nanak's *bani* is a great gift. I get up early in the morning and recite *gurbani*; Guru Nanak blesses me with his *darshan*. Guru Nanak has blessed this family with the gift of a son. I am just a messenger of Guru Nanak, who uses my voice to bless this family.

Shabad-Kirtan (Hymn Singing)

Shabad-kirtan is an integral part of the Sikh service, which begins with hymn singing from the scripture. It is usually performed by a group of *ragis* (religious musicians). The tradition of *shabad-kirtan* was introduced by Guru Nanak, who composed his *bani* (compositions) in poetic form, while his companion Mardana, a Muslim minstrel, provided the musical setting, and then they sang together. Like Guru Nanak, his successors had Muslim musicians called *rababis*, who performed *shabad-kirtan* for them.

Today, the *Shiromani Gurdwara Parbandhak Committee* employs professional Sikh *ragis* to perform *shabad-kirtan* at historic *gurdwaras*. Most community-based *gurdwaras* employ full-time *granthis*, who usually perform *shabad-kirtan* as well. They also teach music to Sikh children at the *gurdwaras*. The descendants of Bhai Mardana are treated most respectfully by the Sikh community. They are invited by the Sikhs to perform at important celebrations in India as well as abroad. The *shabad-kirtan* plays an important role in transmitting the message of the *gurbani* (scriptures) to the *sangat*.

The tradition of *rein sabai kirtan* (all-night singing) is very popular among Sikhs. It is similar to the traditional *jagrata* (all-night singing of hymns dedicated to the Mother Goddess) in the Hindu tradition. Usually, the officials of a *gurdwara* organize *rein sabai kirtan* once or twice a year. It begins at 7:00 P.M. and comes to an end in the early hours of the morning. A relay of *ragis* take part in the *rein sabai kirtan*. *Langar* is prepared for the *sangat* and is served all night. Sometimes individual Sikh families prepare the *langar* for the *sangat*, which is regarded as *sewa*.

Sat Sang in Sikh Homes

The term *sat sang* literally means "the company of holy persons," and is reverently used for *shabad-kirtan* sessions. Most devout Sikh families organize *sat sang* at their homes, where they invite local *ragis* to perform the *shabad-kirtan*. A *sat sang* usually lasts two to three hours and ends with a Sikh prayer and a communal meal prepared by the family. Another interesting development is the popularity of "Ladies' Sat Sang." It is primarily a women's gathering, where Sikh ladies perform hymn singing. They are usually held at the *gurdwaras*, but sometimes Sikh families organize Ladies' Sat Sang at private homes. The *shabad-kirtan* is performed by Sikh women, most of whom are amateur singers; they also participate in the *shabad-kirtan* at *gurdwaras*.

Karah-Parshad (Sanctified Food)

Karah-parshad is the most important food and is distributed to members of the *sangat* at the culmination of the service. It is regarded as a gift from God and is always received in cupped hands. The term *karah-parshad* is composed of two words: *karah*, meaning an iron pan, and *parshad*, denoting food offered to a deity (hence, sanctified food cooked in an iron pan). The word *parshad* also means "grace," signifying the sacredness of the food. Another word applied to *karah-parshad* is *deg* (literally, a cooking pot).

Preparation of the *karah-parshad* is regarded as a sacred ritual. The kitchen must be clean. Usually, it is cooked by a *granthi*, who takes a bath before beginning the preparations. He or she recites *gurbani* (compositions from the Adi Granth) during the entire operation, and no one is allowed to interfere during preparation of the *karah-parshad*.

Once the *karah-parshad* is ready, it is carried above the head to the congregational hall and placed near the Adi Granth. During recital of the *ardas*, a special plea is made for God's blessing of *karah-parshad*. At that moment, an attendant stirs the *karah-parshad* with a small sword, signifying fulfillment of the plea. Before the *karah-parshad* is distributed to members of the congregation it is ritually offered to five *amritdhari* (initiated) Sikhs, symbolizing the authority of the guru. No Sikh will leave a *gurdwara* without receiving a portion of *karah-parshad* for those members of the family who are not able to visit the *gurdwara*, either because of illness or because they are engaged in domestic duties.

Karah-parshad is made of equal portions of whole-meal flour, sugar, and *ghee* (clarified butter). Many Sikhs make offerings of flour, sugar, and butter to the *gurdwara* for the *karah-parshad*, whereas some families donate cash, particularly for *deg/karah-parshad*.

Ardas (Sikh Prayer)

The term *ardas* is the Punjabi version of the Persian word *arz-dasht*, which is composed of two words: *arz* (plea or request) and *dasht* (to make or to submit)—thus, presenting one's plea or request. The term *ardas* is found in the compositions of Sikh Gurus as recorded in the Adi Granth. The *ardas* is an essential part of Sikh worship. All acts of worship and such ceremonies as weddings, initiation, or *akhand-path* (unbroken reading of the Adi Granth) begin and culminate with an *ardas*.

At the culmination of the service, the whole congregation stands with folded hands for the *ardas*. Mostly, the *granthi* of a *gurdwara* recites the *ardas*, but it can be recited by any Sikh. The present form of an *ardas* is a standardized version approved by the *Shiromani Gurdwara Parbandhak Committee* in 1945. It is believed that the original form of the *ardas* was composed by the tenth Guru, Gobind Singh, whose name is chanted at the start of the recital of an *ardas*.

At the end of the main *ardas*, a short couplet is sung by the whole congregation, which reinforces the belief that all Sikhs are mandated to revere the Adi Granth as their Guru, culminating in a Sikh slogan: "*Wahey Guru ji ka Khalsa, Wahey Guru Ji ki Fateh*" (the *Khalsa* belongs to God and victory is to God). The congregation then sits down and awaits the *hukamnama*. The *granthi* opens the Adi Granth in a random fashion and recites the first hymn on the left-hand page, which is regarded as the Guru's order for the day. The service ends with distribution of *karah-parshad* to every member of the congregation.

6

Growing Up Sikh

I am neither a child, a young man,
nor an ancient; nor am I of any caste.

—Guru Nanak

P unjabi/Sikh society is patriarchal in authority, and all inheritance passes through the male line, which ensures the continuity of one's lineage. The basic unit is the joint household, usually a three-generation unit comprising grandparents, married sons and their wives and children, and unmarried sons and daughters. Property is held by the head of the family for common use, and economic resources are pooled together. Roles within the family structure are clearly defined, with the emphasis on subordination of personal ambition to family interests. Upholding one's family honor (*izzat*) is the primary obligation of all members.

The Sikh family functions like a large social services department. Child-rearing, education, marriage, and general care are the responsibility of the family. Children learn by example rather than by training. They grow up as members of the joint household rather than belonging only to their biological parents. In the case of death of the adult members of a family, children are brought up by their mother's family. A child never loses the support of the extended kinship network. There has been no tradition of childcare by government agencies like social services. A childless couple will usually adopt a male child of their close relatives with a view to facilitating transfer of property. It is important to note that before the Hindu Succession Act of 1956, Hindu and Sikh women had no right to inherit property from either their fathers or husbands.

BIRTH

There has been much sharing of cultural traditions between Hindus and Sikhs in the Punjab. They observe the same rules of social organization, caste, and rites of passage. In Punjabi/Sikh society, the birth of a child is regarded as a *parmatma di daat* (gift of God). After marriage, the birth of a child is eagerly awaited by the parents of the young couple. Upon the birth of a son, there is much rejoicing and exchanging of gifts, while the arrival of a daughter remains a comparatively quiet affair. For the birth of a son, the main door of the house is decorated with leaves from a *sirin* (*Arcacia sirissa*) or a mango tree, which symbolizes the superior status of a male child. Moreover, the festival of *Lohrdi* is exclusively celebrated on the birth of a boy. The family distributes sweets and roasted peanuts among relatives and members of one's *biradari* (caste). During the evening, a huge bonfire is prepared to which the women of the *biradari* are invited to sing songs celebrating the birth of the boy. The festival of *Lohrdi* is very popular among Sikhs in the United Kingdom.

At the birth of a child, both mother and child remain secluded for thirteen days. The mother is forbidden to enter the kitchen because she is regarded as ritually polluted after giving birth. On the thirteenth day, she has a ritual bath. Her old clothes are discarded, which, along with some food, are received by the midwife as her ritual payment. The tradition in the United Kingdom is quite different from that in the Punjab, and the process of adaptation to the new environment has been remarkably rapid. In the United Kingdom, childbirth takes place in a hospital, and most mothers do not have the support of a traditional joint/extended family. In addition, the notion of pollution associated with childbirth has lost its ritual significance for second-generation Sikhs.

RITUAL OF CHHATTI

Another important ceremony that usually takes place five weeks after the birth of a son is called *Chhatti*. This is a big feast organized by the paternal family to which the mother's parents, other relatives, and members of the *biradari* are invited. The mother and child receive gifts, including a small amount of cash, called a *sagan* (auspicious gift). The festivals of *Lohrdi* and *Chhatti* are instrumental in reinforcing and perpetuating patriarchal values. In the diaspora, most Sikh families celebrate the ritual of *Chhatti* at the *gurdwaras*, and a ritual reading of the Adi Granth is normally organized as part of the celebration.

The birth of a girl is regarded as a constant reminder of her transient membership in the birth family and that she will one day join her husband's household. At her wedding, the father performs the ritual of *kanyadan* (gift of the virgin to the husband) to gain the highest merit. She virtually remains a *prayee* (outsider) in her parents' household and is also regarded as a financial liability because of the cost of her dowry and wedding. In the past, it was a tradition to entertain a wedding party for three days.

In Punjabi/Sikh society, boys and girls are prepared for distinct roles within the family. While a girl learns to cook and sew, as well as look after younger brothers and sisters, a boy is trained to take up his father's role by pursuing outdoor activities. In the past, formal education was exclusively financed for sons only; this was regarded as an important investment in the family's fortune. A girl was constantly reminded of her future role as a wife in her husband's house, and her behavior as an ideal wife would enhance the honor of her parents.

This situation has radically changed since India gained independence from Great Britain in 1947. Girls are now encouraged to go to university, and their educational achievement is regarded as a significant factor for a good marriage. The Sikh community in the diaspora has shown a remarkable capacity for adaptation and change. Nowadays, both girls and boys are encouraged to receive university education and get good jobs. Second- and third-generation Sikh women are creatively engaged in extending the boundaries of gender equality.

NAMING

Children are traditionally given names by their grandparents. Most Sikh families now go to the *gurdwara* and ask for an initial letter from the Adi Granth to help choose a name. In the United Kingdom, a name is usually obtained directly after the Sunday service. The first letter of the first word of the *hukamnama* (order of the day) hymn is used for the child's name. The *hukamnama* is the recital of a randomly chosen hymn from the Adi Granth after the final *ardas*. The selected name is usually announced at the *gurdwara*. Devout Sikh families ensure that a newborn baby receives *amrit* (ritually prepared water). The *granthi* (official reader of the scriptures) recites the first five verses of the Adi Granth while stirring the mixture of water and sugar with a *Khanda* (small double-edged sword). He then puts some *amrit* into the baby's mouth with a *kirpan* (miniature ceremonial sword). Most first names are popular for both boys and girls. For example, Mohinder, Surjeet, and Sukhvinder are Sikh first names for boys and girls. In order to distinguish between male and female names, the title "Singh" or "Kaur" is added to the first name; for example, Mohinder Kaur is a girl's name, while Mohinder Singh would signify a male.

PAGRI BANANAN (TYING OF THE TURBAN CEREMONY)
A turban is an essential part of a male Sikh uniform. It is also worn by many Muslims and Hindus on the Indian subcontinent. It is both a garment and a symbol of honor. A Sikh boy begins to wear a turban at the age of eleven or twelve when, in fact, he is able to look after it, but there is no specific age requirement.

GURU NANAK CELEBRATES GENDER EQUALITY AS THE "DIVINE GIFT":

Of woman are we born, of woman conceived
To woman engaged, to woman married.
Woman we befriend, by woman do civilizations continue.
When a woman dies, a woman is sought for.
It is through woman that order is maintained.
Then why call her inferior from whom
all great ones are born?
Woman is born of woman;
None is born but of a woman.
The One, who is Eternal, alone is unborn.
Says Nanak, that tongue alone is blessed
That utters the praise of the One.
Such alone will be acceptable at the Court of the True One.*

* Adi Granth, 473.

Many Sikh families presently organize a *pagri bananan* ceremony, which is usually performed at a *gurdwara*. After the recital of an *ardas* (Sikh prayer) the *granthi* or an elderly male is invited to tie the turban on the boy's head. A turban is normally made of muslin cloth and is five yards in length. They may be of any color, but elderly Sikhs prefer to wear white turbans. Members of the Akali Party (the political party of the Sikhs) wear blue turbans, while saffron is popular with the *Khalsa*. Members of the Namdhari sect and the Guru Nanak Nishkam Sewak Jatha organization wear white turbans. A small number of Sikh women, followers of Sant Randhir Singh, also wear turbans. Interestingly, they also wear traditional *dupatta* (long scarves) over their turbans. White American Sikh converts, popularly known as members of 3HO (the Healthy, Happy, Holy Organization), wear white turbans irrespective of gender.

Sikh migrant workers fought for the right to wear turbans at work in Britain, the United States, and Canada. In the United Kingdom, turbaned Sikhs have been exempted from wearing helmets while riding bikes. At present, Sikhs in France are actively engaged in a campaign for the right of children to wear turbans at school.

MARRIAGE

The vehicle for the transition from childhood to adulthood in Punjabi/Sikh society is the institution of marriage. Marriage is also regarded as the bedrock of Sikh society. Guru Nanak strongly rejected the practice of asceticism and celibacy. He taught his followers that they should lead the normal life of householders; recognizing their obligations to parents, spouse, and children, and to the wider society.

A Sikh wedding has far greater significance than the simple unification of a man and woman in the matrimonial state; it is regarded as an alliance between two families of compatible social and caste status. A wedding is both a social and religious occasion. The concept of *sanjog* (a relationship preordained by God) plays an important role in the establishment of a marriage alliance. The Sikh scriptures consider marriage to be a spiritual bond; they emphasize the concept of *ek jote doye murti* (one soul in two bodies).

Pre-wedding and wedding rituals provide meaningful insight into the complex network of kinship ties, the entanglement of religion with social structure, and the functioning of caste. Traditionally, marriages are arranged by parents. In the past, it was customary to arrange marriages when children were very young. Marriages are now arranged when children complete their education. Marital alliances are established according to the rules of caste endogamy, according to which "correct" partners can be found in one's own caste group, so that a Jat Sikh marries a Jat, while a Ramgarhia Sikh marries a Ramgarhia. Since the institution of marriage plays an important part in maintaining boundaries between caste groups, inter-caste marriages are strongly disapproved of, and the partners in such relationships are treated as outsiders and a stain on the family honor.

The process of arranging marriage begins when the parents ask their relatives to look for a suitable spouse for a son or daughter. A person who arranges the *rishta* (marital alliance) is called a *bichola* (matchmaker). In the past, the role of a matchmaker was performed by the family *nai* (barber). Marriage negotiations are conducted in complete secrecy to avoid any family embarrassment. In the past, families relied soley upon the matchmaker. Nowadays, the parents meet both the girl and the boy, and also arrange a meeting between the spouses in order to seek their approval before the final decision to proceed with the engagement ceremony.

The engagement ceremony is one of the most important pre-wedding rituals; it is performed at the boy's residence or at a local *gurdwara*. A party of five or seven kinsmen of the girl, usually her father and his brothers, take part in the engagement ceremony, which takes place in the presence of male relatives and members of one's *biradari*. It begins with the recital of an *ardas* and reading of the hymn of *kurmai* (engagement) from the Adi Granth. Then the girl's father puts seven handfuls of dried fruit in the boy's *jholi* (lap made from a pink scarf) and then puts one *chhuara* (dried date) in the boy's mouth. This ritual is called *sagan dena* (offering of a ritual gift), and it confirms the establishment of the relationship. Usually the boy receives gifts of a golden *kara* (bracelet) and some cash from the girl's father.

Pre-Wedding Rituals
Sahey Chithi (Ritual Invitation)
It is customary to send a *sahey chithi* (invitation letter) to the boy's family, formally inviting them to the solemnization of the marriage on the appointed day. The *sahey chithi* is prepared in the presence of close relatives and members of the *biradari*, and it is sprinkled with saffron. This custom has a ritual significance, because red is believed to be the symbol for renewal of life. In the past, it was the customary duty of the family *nai* (barber) to deliver the *sahey chithi*, for which he received a ritual gift of clothes and some cash. Today, a *sahey chithi* is delivered by the matchmaker.

Mayian
Pre-wedding rituals signify the continuity and practice of centuries-old Indic cultural traditions and their impact on Punjabi/Sikh society. The term *mayian* denotes ritual rubbing of a paste made of tumeric (a spice), flour, and mustard oil on a boy/girl's face, arms, and legs, performed at their respective homes. The prospective bride or groom is seated on a wooden plank called a *patri*, which is provided by the family carpenter, for which he receives his ritual gift of cooked food. A red cloth is held above by four female relatives while married women of the household and *biradari*, led by the mother, perform the ritual of rubbing the paste. During this ritual, women sing traditional songs and receive the ritual gift of *gogley* (Punjabi sweet specially cooked for weddings) at the end.

Chura

One day before the wedding, the ritual of *chura* (a set of multi-colored ivory bangles) is performed at the bride's residence. Her maternal uncle makes a gift of clothes, jewelry, and some cash called the *nankey-shak*. He puts the bangles on his niece while the women sing traditional songs describing the role of the maternal uncle. The girl gets wed in clothes provided by her maternal uncle. Similarly, the bridegroom receives a set of clothes, called the *jora lama*, from his maternal uncle, which he wears at the wedding ceremony. This ritual emphasizes the importance of the role of the mother's natal family at wedding rituals.

Milni

The ceremony of *milni*—a declaration of the alliance of the two families—is the most important pre-wedding ritual. The term *milni* literally means a ceremonial meeting of the heads of two families. It begins with recital of the *ardas*, and then the fathers of the bride and groom are invited to shake hands; the bride's father then makes a ritual gift of one turban and some cash to the groom's father. Similarly, the bride's maternal uncle makes a ritual gift of one turban and some cash to his counterpart. The ritual of *milni* is restricted to those kinsmen who are related to the family through blood and marriage. Friends of the groom's family do not receive gifts, which signifies the nature of the ritual of *milni* as a boundary line between kin and other relationships.

Anand Karaj (Wedding Ceremony)

It is mandatory to perform the *anand karaj* in the presence of the Adi Granth. The bride and groom sit in front of the Adi Granth, and the ceremony begins with recital of the *ardas* followed by the ritual of *palla pharana* (joining the couple with the scarf worn by the groom), which is performed by the bride's father. This is a very emotional ritual in which the father gives away his daughter as a *kanyadan* (gift of a virgin). At that moment, the *ragis* (religious musicians) sing the hymn of *palley taindey laagi* from the Adi Granth, which highlights the permanence of the marital bond. The essence of this hymn is a pledge by the bride:

> Praise and blame I forsake both. I hold the edge of your garment/scarf. All else I let pass. All relationships I have found false. I cling to thee my lord. [20]

Lavan (Wedding Hymn)

The ritual of the *palla pharana* is followed by the reading and singing of four verses of the *lavan* (wedding hymn) from the Adi Granth. After the recital of each verse, the couple walk around the Adi Granth in clockwise fashion, the bridegroom leading the bride. This circumambulation is repeated four times. The ceremony of *anand karaj* concludes with recital of the hymn *anand sahib* and an *ardas*.

At a Namdhari Sikh wedding, the bride and groom walk around the *havan* (holy fire) while the verses of *lavan* are recited from the Adi Granth. In the past, Sikh brides, like their Hindu counterparts, covered their faces during the wedding ceremony. But Namdhari Sikh leaders reformed the tradition of *purdah* (covering one's face) at the wedding ceremony, as well as in public.

DIETARY CODE

Sikh Gurus emphasized the virtues of vegetarianism and the vices of intoxicants, so many Sikhs, particularly men, do not eat meat or consume alcohol. Sikh women are traditionally vegetarian and refrain from drinking alcohol and smoking as well; however, the attitude of educated women has radically changed. The rapid increase in alcoholism among male Sikhs in India and abroad is troubling for the community in general and the families in particular.

According to the rules of the *Rahit Maryada* (the Sikh code of discipline), a Sikh should not partake of alcohol or intoxicants, or use tobacco. Sikhs are also prohibited from eating *halal* (meat slaughtered according to Muslim tradition), and do not eat beef, maintaining this essentially Indic tradition. It is important to note that all food cooked and served at *gurdwaras* is vegetarian. *Amritdhari* (initiated) Sikhs are prohibited from eating meat, consuming alcohol or taking drugs, and smoking.

Traditionally, no meat—regarded as demon food—was cooked or served at weddings, but meat and alcohol are now the most popular items on a Sikh wedding menu.

DOLI (RITUAL DEPARTURE OF
THE BRIDE WITH HER HUSBAND)

In the past, the bride was carried in a *doli* (a kind of sedan) to the husband's home by four *jheers* (water-carrier caste) men. A modern bride and groom leave in a car, so that the traditional role of water-carrier has become dated. The ritual of *doli torna* symbolizes permanent change in the bride's status from being a member of her father's household to being a member of her husband's family.

MUKLAWA

The consummation of the marriage is called *muklawa*. In the past, a few years would elapse between wedding and *muklawa*, depending on the age of the couple. Today, it usually takes place a day after the wedding. The daughter then departs permanently from her parental home to join her husband's household, where her major role is to produce sons to be her husband's heirs and who will continue his lineage. In years past, there was not a traditional "honeymoon" in Punjabi culture, but most couples now go away for a honeymoon.

DOWRY (DAAJ)

The issue of a dowry is problematic for Sikhs. Although the Sikh *Rahit Maryada* prohibits the giving of dowries, the tradition of a dowry is very popular among Sikhs both in India and in the diaspora. It is regarded as a customary obligation for the bride's parents to provide a substantial amount of clothing, furniture, household goods, and jewelry. In the Sikh diaspora, most brides are working women, and they contribute substantially to their own dowry. In the past, it was customary to display the dowry for the approval of the bridegroom's father and his kin before it was packed up. This practice of dowry display has by now lost virtually all its importance. There is a fundamental difference between the traditional Hindu dowry system and Sikh practice: a Hindu dowry is an amount of cash demanded by the bride-groom's parents to be paid at the end of the wedding ceremony. It is mutually agreed upon and the amount fixed before accept-ance of the marital relationship.

ABORTION AND CONTRACEPTION
The subject of abortion was never discussed publicly in tradi-tional Punjabi society. According to Sikh teachings, life is regarded as a divine gift and thus most sacred. The number and sex of the children to be born into a family is therefore believed to be preordained by God. A childless couple is perceived as *budkismat* (unlucky, suffering from bad deeds done in a previ-ous life). In the event of an unmarried girl becoming pregnant, an abortion is procured secretly to protect the honor of the family. When abortion is prescribed on medical grounds, Sikhs generally follow medical advice. Sikh children born and educated in Western countries believe in family planning, like most of their counterparts.

DIVORCE AND REMARRIAGE
Sikh marriage is regarded as a spiritual relationship and thus cannot be broken. However, in 1955 the Indian Parliament passed the Hindu Marriage Act, which made it permissible for Hindus as well as Sikhs to divorce. Divorce continues to be regarded as a stigma, particularly as a dishonor for the woman and her family. A divorced woman is called a *chhadi hoyi* (discarded woman). In the United Kingdom, Sikhs are governed by the marriage and divorce laws of the land. The rate of divorce is increasing among young Sikhs; although it is very low com-pared to the national average. Generally, Sikh marriages in the diaspora do not fail due to the amount of the dowry.

Sikhs practice remarriage of divorcees and widows. Remarriage of a widow is called *kareva/chador pauna*. In the past, it was common practice to marry the widow of one's elder brother in order to protect the honor of the family. It is a simple ceremony: The groom marries a widow by placing a sheet of cloth (*chador*) over her head in the presence of relatives and members of the *biradari*. A widow is not entitled to a religious wedding because she cannot be given away in the *kanyadan* (gift of a virgin). Young widows move back to their parents, who may arrange remarriage, while widows with children usually stay with their in-laws.

DEATH AND CREMATION

Death is perceived as the ultimate reality by Sikhs. A number of phrases are used to describe the death of a person: *pura ho giya* (completed his/her span of life), *surgwas ho giya* (has taken abode in heaven), *rab da bhana* (Divine Will), and *sansar gatra puri kar giya* (has completed the pilgrimage of this world). Death is not conceived of as the abrupt end of life but as a gradual transition from earthly existence to another state depending on one's performance in this world. Like Hindus, Sikhs believe in the transmigration of the soul. While the human body is cremated, the soul is believed to be immortal.

There are a series of ceremonies that are integral to the funeral ritual called *antam sanskar* (literally, the last rite): the *dharti tey pauna* (lifting of the body from the bed onto the floor), the *antam-ishnan* (last bath), *dhamalak bhanana* (breaking of the earthen pot symbolizing release of the spirit), the *agni bhaint* (ritual offering of one's body to the god of fire), the *pagri* (ritual transfer of paternal authority), and the *akath* (ritual feast).

Antam-ishnan (Last Bath)

In India, funerals usually take place soon after death or the next day, depending on the time of death. The ritual of *antam-ishnan*, performed before the body is carried to the cremation ground, is symbolic of ritual purification of the dead before cremation, which is called *agni bhaint* (offering to the god of fire).

Agni Bhaint

The bier is carried by the sons and brothers of the deceased, led by the chief mourner, the eldest son. The ritual of carrying the bier is called *modha dena* (offering one's shoulder). It is the ritual obligation of a son to light the funeral pyre. In the absence of a son, one of the male relatives performs the ritual lighting of the pyre.

Before lighting the pyre, a *granthi* recites an *ardas* for the departed soul. Women are prohibited from taking part in carrying the bier and from lighting the pyre. In fact, they are not permitted to enter the cremation ground at all.

The ashes are collected after three days and then deposited in the Ganges River at Hardwar or Kiratpur. Ritual gifts of clothes, utensils, and some cash are offered to a family Brahmin for his services, which are donated to a *gurdwara* at Kiratpur.

Pagri (Ritual Transfer of Paternal Authority)

After the funeral, the deceased family organizes the reading of the Adi Granth either at their residence or at a *gurdwara*. The reading of the Adi Granth usually marks the culmination of the thirteen days of mourning, after which a large feast (*akath*) is held for the relatives and members of one's *biradari*.

The ritual of *pagri* (literally, a turban) takes place at the *akath*. The chief mourner sits in front of the Adi Granth and receives a turban and some cash from his maternal uncle. He wears the new turban in the presence of his relatives and members of the *biradari*, discarding the old one. Thereafter, he is reminded of his new status and obligations by a senior member of the *biradari*. He then joins the elders of the *biradari* for a communal meal, having been ritually accepted as the head of the household. The social function of the rite of *pagri* is to facilitate the gradual incorporation of a son into the role of his father.

Widowhood (Randepa)

In Punjabi/Sikh society, a widow is called a *vidhwa* or *randi*. The term *randi* is most abusive: it is used as a swearword for wicked women and prostitutes. The status of widowhood condemns a Sikh woman to a state of perpetual ritual pollution. Her participation in wedding rituals is regarded as inauspicious. At the death of her husband, she discards her colorful clothes and wears a white *chuni* (long scarf) that signifies the status of widowhood and a state of being in mourning.

On the thirteenth day after the death of her husband, she is given a ritual bath by the ladies of the household. She discards her old clothes and wears a new set of clothes provided by her parental family. She discards her white scarf and is ritually incorporated into the family. Interestingly, there are no such prescriptions for Sikh widowers, who are free to marry and have a proper *anand karaj* ceremony.

Let us examine the position of Sikh widows with respect to participation in *gurdwara* activities. The institution of the *gurdwara* is regarded as the house of God, where everyone is treated as equal. A widow is therefore not forbidden from taking part in religious activities at a *gurdwara*. She can participate in preparation of *langar* (communal meal), preparation and distribution of *karah-parshad* (sanctified food distributed to the congregation after a service), and reading of the Adi Granth. In the United Kingdom, many Sikh widows take part in the *shabad-kirtan* (religious singing) and also hold women's *satsang* (religious singing sessions) at *gurdwaras* and Sikh homes. Their participation in religious activities demonstrates the ambivalent attitude of Sikhs in the social and religious domains. While the presence of widows at wedding rituals is perceived as inauspicious, their cooked food is gladly accepted at the *gurdwaras*.

7

Cultural
Expressions

*Even Kings and emperors with
heaps of wealth and vast dominion
cannot compare with an ant
filled with the love of God.*

—Guru Nanak

$\int$ ikh tradition is an inseparable part of the Punjabi cultural heritage that has enriched the life of the Punjabi people over the centuries. Punjabi folk music, dance, and the oral tradition of reciting the legendary stories of heroism of young lovers who challenged tradition have been passed from one generation to the next and have survived despite the tragic division of the Punjab in 1947 between India and Pakistan.

The Sikh movement originated and developed in fifteenth-century Punjab, which was a thoroughfare for invading armies, ideas, and religious traditions—for example, Islam and Persian language, poetry, and dress. Punjabi people welcomed new traditions and embraced them, which facilitated the development of a multifaith/multicultural society. Centuries before Guru Nanak, the Sufi saint Frid composed his poetry in the Punjabi language, which has been included in the Sikh scriptures. With the arrival of Islam, new forms of music and poetry, such as *kawali* and *ghazal*, became popular. The bards and minstrels entertained the common people with tales of love and war in their language, transcending sectarian boundaries.

Guru Nanak rejected the use of Sanskrit and Arabic for his poetry, which he composed in the language of the masses to facilitate transmission of his message of the oneness of God, but he extensively used Persian and traditional Hindu/Indic terms for God and made them part and parcel of daily discourse among ordinary people. He skillfully employed devotional music for congregational worship and, in fact, laid down the foundation for the tradition of *shabad-kirtan*. Most importantly, he chose Mardana, a Muslim minstrel, as his companion during his travels. Guru Nanak composed his *bani* while Mardana set them to music, which they sang together throughout their travels.

Let us take a look at the way the tradition of *shabad-kirtan* emerged as one of the central institutions within the Sikh movement. At the end of his journeys, Guru Nanak settled at Kartarpur, where his disciples would gather at his house early in the morning for congregational worship that began with the *shabad-kirtan*. Guru Nanak was not only a poet but an accomplished musician as well. His successor gurus not only continued the tradition but made it an integral part of the Sikh service. Guru Arjun Dev, compiler of the Adi Granth, put a seal on the musical tradition by setting the scripture to music in thirty-one *ragas* (musical tunes).

The significance of the *shabad-kirtan* is vividly manifested at the Golden Temple, where worship begins with recital and singing of the *Asa di Var*, followed by hymn singing from the Adi Granth, which continues throughout the day. A Sikh service begins with recital and singing of the hymn of *Asa di Var* early in the morning at all *gurdwaras*. It is important to note that most *gurdwaras* conduct music classes for Sikh children, who are encouraged to perform *shabad-kirtan* at Sikh services. Today, both male and female members of the Sikh community take part in *shabad-kirtan* at *gurdwaras*.

The sixth Guru, Hargobind, introduced martial music that was sung at the *Akal Takhat* (the throne of the Timeless God); built by him for the purpose of discussing the political and social concerns of the Sikhs. He employed two Muslim bards, called *dhadis* (musicians who play the *dhad*, a double-headed drum). A number of Sikh musical groups now specialize in martial music. They are often invited to perform at the *gurdwaras* of the diaspora. They display their skill and expand on the martial tradition of the Sikh movement, and also relate historical episodes. They represent traditional folk music blended with the religious and cultural traditions of the Sikh movement.

British colonial rule in the Punjab had a dramatic impact on the Sikh community. According to the 1868 census, Sikhs were a small minority in the Punjab, numbering 1,144,090 (6.5 percent) of a total of just over 17,000,000. The overwhelming majority of the Sikh community lived in the rural Punjab and were mainly agriculturists, skilled artisans, and landless laborers. Their cultural needs were fulfilled by a number of traditional specialists—for example, holy men, bards, and family Brahmins—who presided over the main rites of passage. The festival of

Sangrand, the first day of the month, was a very important day in the life of the village; when the family Brahmani (wife of a Brahmin) would visit, proclaim the name of the auspicious day, and narrate traditional stories. She would receive traditional payment in kind—for example, raw sugar or a jar of wheat grain.

MARTYRDOM IN SIKH TRADITION

The notion of martyrdom and the role of martyrs play a major role in transmitting Sikh religious and cultural values. Most *gurdwaras* maintain libraries that provide storybooks depicting the heroic past of the Sikh movement. Most libraries usually display pictures of Sikh martyrs, like Guru Arjun Dev, Guru Teg Bahadur, the youngest sons of Guru Gobind Singh, Baba Dip Singh holding his severed head while injured during the battle of the defense of the Golden Temple, and persecution of the Sikhs by the Mughal authorities. Let us closely examine the nature of torture depicted in these pictures. Guru Arjun Dev is shown sitting on a red-hot iron plate; other pictures show him being immersed in boiling water, and in another his torturer is pouring hot sand over his head. The picture of Guru Gobind Singh's sons depicts the scene of their death at Sirhand. It is believed that they were buried alive. The manner of their execution is extremely barbaric: both young boys are shown being bricked into a wall, but they are portrayed as perfectly calm and collected. These pictures are a major channel for transmission of the Sikh heritage.

The significance of the role of martyrs in Sikh religious and political history constitutes a major component in discourse among Sikhs worldwide. All Sikh martyrs are reverentially remembered during the recital of the *ardas*. The text of the *ardas* recalls the sacrifice of those who gave their lives to uphold the principles of Sikh *Dharm/a*. It reads as follows:

> Those Sikh men and women who gave their heads for their faith, who were hacked limb from limb, scalped, broken on the wheel and sawn asunder; who sacrificed their lives for

The Golden Temple at Amritsar is the principal house of worship for Sikhs and is known as *Harimandir Sahib*, which literally means the "Temple of God." Founded by Guru Ram Das in the late sixteenth century, the temple was completed in 1604 by his youngest son, Guru Arjan Dev. The temple was destroyed in the 1760s by Afghan invaders but was rebuilt and its golden domes and marble walls were added in the early nineteenth century.

Guru Nanak Dev, portrayed here in a miniature portrait on ivory that is displayed at the Victoria and Albert Museum in London, is the first Guru and founder of Sikhism. Guru Nanak was born into the Hindu Khatri caste (merchants) in 1469 in the Punjab. He developed a deep interest in finding the meaning and purpose of life, and he traveled for a number of years before settling in Kartarpur, Punjab. It was here that Guru Nanak professed his beliefs in the oneness of God and that meditation must be inward. Thus he rejected all outward reflections, including temples, idols, and scriptures.

This woodcutting of the ten Gurus is displayed at the Victoria and Albert Museum in London. The Gurus were the first ten leaders of the Sikh faith, beginning with Guru Nanak and ending with Gobind Singh in 1708. During the time of the first five Gurus (1469–1606), many Sikh traditions were established, including human guruship, congregational worship, the langar (communal meal), compilation of the Adi Granth, and the Golden Temple.

Ranjit Singh established the Punjabi/Sikh state in 1799 and proclaimed himself maharaja, or ruler, of the Punjab in 1801. Under Singh's leadership, the Punjab experienced a fifty-year period of peace and prosperity until the British annexed the area in 1849. This miniature painting is on display at the Musée national des Arts Asiatiques-Guimet in Paris.

The Golden Throne of Maharaja Ranjit Singh, on display at the Victoria and Albert Museum, London. The throne is made of wood and resin, and is covered with sheets of embossed gold.

Gobind Singh, the tenth Guru, and the panj pyarey, or five beloved ones, are portrayed here partaking in the Sikh ceremony known as amrit, which initiated the group into the Sikh religious order of Khalsa. The group was not only elevated to the warrior and princely caste but women were admitted into the Khalsa, thus reinforcing the Sikh belief in the equality of humankind.

A Baisakhi procession led by the panj pyarey (beloved five), symbolizing the original members of the Khalsa.

Harbhajan Singh Puri, popularly known as Yogi Bhajan, was instrumental in helping to spread Sikhism to the West. In 1971, Puri founded the 3HO movement, which stands for "Healthy, Happy, Holy Organization." The group espouses meditation, improvement of physical well-being, and a deepening spiritual awareness.

The fifth Guru, Arjun Dev, collected the writings of his predecessors and compiled the Adi Granth (shown here), which he completed in 1604. The Adi Granth is the central object of worship in Sikh temples and contains the Mul Mantra (basic creed), Japji (the hymn written by Guru Nanak), and other hymns that provide insight into Sikh beliefs, especially the concept of the oneness of God.

the protection of gurdwaras, never forsaking their faith;
and who were steadfast in their loyalty to the uncut hair:
remember their pious deeds by loudly uttering *Waheyguru*
(Wonderful God).[21]

It is important to note that the *ardas* is recited at the culmination of every Sikh service and individual act of worship at home.
The memory of Sikh martyrs is a constant reminder of a heroic
past, which is transmitted to Sikh children all over the world.

Pictures of Sikh Gurus, Sikh martyrs, and historical *gurdwaras*
are today printed for mass distribution. Some publishers print
these pictures on yearly calendars. They are sold in shops as well
as at *gurdwaras*. Another major channel of transmission of Sikh
ideals is the display of the weapons of Guru Gobind Singh and
other Sikh leaders. After recital of the hymn of *arti*, the weapons
of Guru Gobind Singh are reverently displayed for the congregation by one of the officiants at the Nanded gurdwara. He
handles each weapon with utmost reverence and comments on
their history, after which the weapons are taken to their special
room. Moreover, almost all historic *gurdwaras* associated with
the tenth Guru, Gobind Singh, have traditional weapons laid
out in front of the Adi Granth in the main congregation hall,
where Sikh officiants meticulously comment on each weapon
for the benefit of the *sangat*.

Every year, martyrdom-day anniversaries of Sikh Gurus are
celebrated by Sikhs throughout the world. A martyrdom-day
gurpurb (anniversary) begins with the ritual of *akhand-path*
(unbroken reading of the Adi Granth that takes forty-eight
hours), which culminates in a Sikh service. On the martyrdom-
day of fifth Guru Arjun Dev, special stalls are installed where
soft drinks are offered to members of the public, signifying
the importance of the Guru's sacrifice to uphold the principle
of "Divine Will." Sikh youngsters enthusiastically take part in
serving the drinks. Sikh *ragis* and preachers reflect upon the
grand narrative of martyrdom in general and Guru Arjun Dev's
martyrdom in particular.

In 1984, Sant Jarnail Singh Bhinderanwaley, the charismatic militant leader, launched his campaign for the establishment of *Khalistan* (an independent Sikh state) from the *Akal Takhat.* The Indian army eventually attacked the *Akal Takhat* to dislodge him and his followers. Ironically, the attack coincided with the martyrdom-day anniversary of the fifth Guru. A large number of Sikhs had thus gathered in the Golden Temple complex for the annual celebrations. Unfortunately, the military action resulted in considerable loss of life among both Sikhs and soldiers. The *Akal Takhat* was virtually destroyed, and Sant Bhinderanwaley and his close advisors were also killed during the operation.

Sant Bhinderanwaley and his advisors are reverently remembered today as Sikh martyrs by many Sikhs. Many *gurdwaras* in the diaspora hold special services remembering Sant Bhinderanwaley and his associates. The details of such services are advertised in the Punjabi press, along with pictures of Sant Bhinderanwaley and the badly destroyed *Akal Takhat.* The speakers and musicians at these services emphasize the tradition of martyrdom within the Sikh movement and encourage young Sikhs to become *amritdhari* (initiated).

The Sikh Martyr of Vancouver
In the early twentieth century, approximately seven thousand Sikhs immigrated to Canada. In 1907, the Sikh community in Vancouver established the Khalsa Diwan Society to fight against

MARTYRDOM

Highlighting the essence of the concept of martyrdom, Guru Nanak said:

If you want to play the game of love
approach me with your head on the palm
of your hand. Place your feet on this
path and give your head without regard
to the opinion of others.*

* Adi Granth, 1,412.

racial discrimination. They set out to build their *gurdwara*, which was completed in 1909 and became their central institution, serving their social and religious needs. The *gurdwara* emerged as the vanguard to unite the community against discrimination and draconian immigration rules. The notorious episode of the *Kamagata Maru* occurred in 1914, when the ship docked in the port of Vancouver. On board were 376 Indian passengers, 346 of whom were Sikhs. Canadian immigration authorities refused to allow the passengers to disembark. The Sikh community in Vancouver collected funds for the necessary harbor fee during two months of negotiations, but the *Kamagata Maru* was ultimately forced to leave port.

In a graphic account of what transpired after the departure of the *Kamagata Maru*, Khushwant Singh recorded:

> In Vancouver, a trail of violence followed the departure of the *Kamagata Maru*. The immigration department had engaged the services of a eurasian policeman, William Hopkinson, to break the Ghadar (Revolution) organisation. Hopkinson's chief aide was one Bela Singh. Two of Bela Singh's henchmen were found murdered. At the post-funeral service of these murdered men in the gurdwara, Bela Singh killed two and wounded six other men. William Hopkinson volunteered to appear as a witness for the defence in the trial of Bela Singh. On October 21, 1914, Hopkinson was shot and killed by Mewa Singh, the priest (*granthi*) of the gurdwara. Mewa Singh was sentenced to death. Prior to his execution he made a confessional statement which ran: "My religion does not teach me to bear enmity with anybody, no matter what class, creed or order he belongs to, nor had I any enmity with Hopkinson. I heard that he was oppressing my poor people very much ... I—being a staunch Sikh—could no longer bear to see the wrong done both to my innocent countrymen and the Dominion of Canada ... shall gladly have the rope put around my neck thinking it to be rosary of God's name." [22]

The martyrdom of Mewa Singh contributed to the reinforcement of the Sikh community's resolve to unite against the
racial policies of Canadian authorities. The Sikhs of Vancouver
now celebrate Mewa Singh's martyrdom every March in the
Khalsa Diwan Society's *gurdwara*, and these celebrations are
attended by many Californian Sikhs.

SOCIAL STRUCTURE IN PUNJABI/SIKH CULTURE

The development of Punjabi/Sikh arts and crafts is closely
linked to the social structure of Punjabi society. It is therefore
important that we proceed to locate it within its proper historical context. The Sikh movement originated and developed
in the context of a caste-based Hindu society where caste
status was ascribed on the basis of one's birth into a particular
caste, which was closely linked to one's traditional occupation.
The son of a carpenter inherited his occupation and his caste
identity from his parents. Moreover, it was one's *dharma* to marry
within one's caste. Each caste had a council (*panchayat*),
which was responsible for enforcing caste *dharma*. This is
how the boundaries of the caste system were clearly marked
and defended. There was in fact no social mobility within the
caste structure.

Caste still remains an important aspect of Punjabi/Sikh society
despite its rejection by the Sikh Gurus. The Jat Sikhs dominate
numerically, politically, and economically in Punjabi villages.
They control the land and its use, while all other serving caste
groups work for them. Interestingly, Jat Sikhs emerged as the
backbone of the Sikh movement under the leadership of the Sikh
Gurus. Baba Buddha, a Jat Sikh, was the first *granthi* appointed
after compilation of the Adi Granth in 1604. After the execution
of Banda Bahadur in 1716, Sikhs organized themselves into
twelve *misls* (armies); all but one of which was led by Jat Sikhs. In
1799, a charismatic Jat Sikh leader, Ranjit Singh, captured Lahore
and established the sovereign state of the Punjab. The rulers of all
princely states in the Punjab were Jat Sikhs. During British rule,
Jat Sikh soldiers played a key role in the British army.

In postindependence India, Jat Sikhs have held top positions in the Indian armed forces. They have also emerged as a dominant force within political and religious institutions in the Punjab. In the 1960s, the agricultural output of the Punjab increased enormously under the energetic leadership of Jat Sikh farmers, which greatly helped to solve India's food problem. This came to be known as the "Green Revolution." Interestingly, the road transport industry in the Punjab is also virtually controlled by the Jat Sikhs.

CONTRIBUTION OF PUNJABI/SIKH CRAFTSMEN

Punjabi/Sikh craftsmanship is vividly reflected in the magnificent architecture throughout the Punjab, including the Golden Temple, the *bungas* (mansions of Sikh leaders) near the Golden Temple, the beautiful buildings at Khalsa College, Amritsar, and the royal courts and palaces of Lahore. During British rule, large numbers of Punjabi/Sikh craftsmen were recruited as indentured servants, who played a key role in the development of the East African colonies. Modern Kenya, Uganda, and Tanzania are living examples of their unparalleled contribution.

Let us take note of the biographical sketch of one such craftsman, Ram Singh, who was born into a Ramgarhia family in the mid-nineteenth century. He worked in a woodcarver's shop

KABIR CRITIQUE OF CASTE SYSTEM

The Indian mystic Kabir, like the Sikh Gurus, was highly critical of the caste system and challenges the Brahmins for claiming superior caste status. He stated:

> There is no clan or caste while dwelling in the womb. Everything is created from the seed of God. Tell me *Pandit* [Brahmin], when were the Brahmins created? Do not waste your life by proclaiming the *Brahminhood*. If you are a Brahmin, born of a Brahmin woman, why have not come through an other way?*

* Adi Granth, 324.

in Amritsar, where he attracted the attention of John Lockwood Kipling (father of Rudyard Kipling), the first principal of Mayo School of Industrial Arts in Lahore. Ram Singh attended Mayo School as a student and went on to join the faculty after successfully completing his studies. As Mr. Kipling's assistant, he designed new buildings for the town's museum and Technical Institute, and the Mayo School of Industrial Arts.

In 1890, Ram Singh received an invitation to travel to London and participate in an international exhibition, and also to prepare an architectural design for the Darbar Hall wing in the Royal Palace. His work was highly appreciated by European architects. He was even granted a special audience with Queen Victoria. After his trip to England, Ram Singh became principal of the Mayo School of Industrial Arts and was awarded the titles "Sardar Sahib" and "Sardar Bahadur" in 1909 and "Member of Victoria Order" in 1911. He designed a number of buildings, the most prominent of which were the Indian Darbar Hall, Aitchison Chiefs' College, the Senate Hall of Punjab University, Foreman Christian College (Lahore), and the Lady Aitchison Hospital. In 1911, he prepared the architectural and interior design schemes for the Coronation Hall in Delhi that were used at the royal ceremonies in honor of King George V. Ram Singh died at a relatively young age in 1916.

ORIGIN OF THE TITLE RAMGARHIA

The story of the origin of the title *Ramgarhia* is a noteworthy part of Sikh history. Punjabi craftsmen traditionally include carpenters, blacksmiths, and bricklayers. As previously mentioned, after the death of Banda Bahadur in 1716, the Sikhs organized themselves into twelve *misls* (armies). One of the *misls* was led by Jassa Singh of the *Tarkhan* caste. Ironically, there was another *misl* leader called Jassa Singh who belonged to the *Ahluwalia* caste. Jassa Singh *Tarkhan* built the fort of Ramgarh for the defense of the Golden Temple. He was then put in charge of defending the Golden Temple by Sikh leaders. It was as governor of the fort of Ramgarh that he came to be known as Jassa Singh Ramgarhia, a title bestowed upon him by the leaders of the Sikh *misls*. Since then, Sikh craftsmen have proudly adopted the title Ramgarhia and are now known as Ramgarhia Sikhs.

FOLK MUSIC AND DANCE IN PUNJABI/SIKH CULTURE

Music and dance had been the traditional occupations of such caste groups as minstrels, bards, and dancing/singing girls (popularly known as *kanjarian*, literally prostitutes). The wider Punjabi society had been entertained by these specialist groups for centuries. The profession of music and dance had a very low status in traditional Punjabi/Sikh culture and was called *kanjarian da dhanda* (profession of prostitutes). It was Guru Nanak who introduced the tradition of *shabad-kirtan* and transformed the status of devotional music.

Despite the traditional attitude of disapproval of music and dance, Punjabi people had long been enjoying folk music/dance that was popularly known as *bhangra* and *giddha*. *Bhangra* is the most popular Punjabi folk dance and is usually performed at the festival of *Baisakhi*. A group of six to eight young men in colorful dress take part in the dance, which is performed to the beat of a *dhole* (large double-headed drum) that sets the tune and speed. One member of the *bhangra* team sings folk music called *bolian*, depicting heroic tales of the Punjab. *Bhangra* dance has become extremely popular in the Punjab and the Sikh diaspora. Professional *bhangra* groups are invited to perform at Sikh/Punjabi weddings. In 1997, the *Nachda Punjab Bhangra* group performed *bhangrara* in honor of Queen Elizabeth during her visit to Bradford, England. Men and women guests jointly perform *bhangra*, which is accompanied by Punjabi folk music at wedding receptions.

Giddha

Giddha is a traditional Punjabi folk dance performed exclusively by women. In the past, *giddha* was performed after a wedding party had moved to the bride's village. Women were prohibited from joining the wedding party and instead performed *giddha* and sang folk songs. Sometimes one or two women would dress up like men and crack racy jokes while pretending to be drunk. Today, the *giddha* dance is performed on the most auspicious family occasions, like the birth of a boy or a house-warming party. In the past, women were prohibited from performing *giddha* in the presence of men but the situation has changed; women now freely participate in the *giddha* dance at wedding receptions and other social functions.

Kavi Darbar (Poetry Reading)
Sikh parents in the diaspora are concerned about retention of the Punjabi language. Poetry reading sessions are becoming very popular, and young Punjabi poets take part and display their skills. A number of young musicians also participate in these sessions. Most Sikh parents and their friends attend to encourage their youngsters. The sessions usually end with a lavish Punjabi meal enjoyed by all present.

Mehndi
Mehndi literally means henna (a reddish-brown dye). In Punjabi culture, *mehndi* is a pre-wedding ritual. A couple of days before the wedding, clan women are invited to the ritual of *mehndi*. Their hands and feet are decorated with *mehndi*, and they sing traditional songs of *sohag* (songs of happily married women). The ceremony of *mehndi* is followed by *giddha* and a lavish meal. At the wedding ceremony, the bride wears a red *bindi* (dot) on her forehead, which is symbolic of a happily married woman. Today, professional *mehndi* decorators are invited to the *mehndi* ritual.

Kalgi
An aigrette (decoration for the head) is called a *kalgi*; it is an ornament for the headgear or turban. A bridegroom wears a *kalgi* at the top of his turban. The *kalgi* is ritually removed before the wedding ceremony. It is a symbolic recognition of the

authority of the Adi Granth. It is important to note that the tenth Guru, Gobind Singh, is affectionately remembered as a *kalgian wala/kalgidhar* (someone who wears *kalgi*) and is always depicted with a *kalgi* in pictures found in *gurdwaras* and Sikh homes. A *kalgi* symbolizes royal status and is normally worn by Indian princes.

Phulkari/Subhar
This is a hand-embroidered shawl made of red (which symbolizes fertility and joy) hand-woven cotton material and embroidered with multicolored silk yarn. It was usually prepared by the mother for her daughter's wedding ceremony. Today, ready-made shawls are worn by brides.

Sherwani
This is a long round-neck coat worn by the bridegroom at a wedding. It is a traditional male garment usually worn by members of royal families. It became extremely popular with the national leaders of India. *Sherwani* is worn with a *pyjama* (similar to a pair of trousers that are narrow at the bottom). Today, all wedding attire and ready-made traditional dresses are sold at stores in Asia.

Influence of Other Cultures
The Punjabi people have displayed an enormous capacity for adaptation and change. Most second- and third-generation Sikh children gladly participate in traditional rituals. Today, traditional Punjabi music mixed with Western tunes is very popular with the younger generation. Members of the younger Sikh generation are entering into such new professions as television presenters, journalists, actors, and film producers. Gurinder Chadha, who directed *Bend It Like Beckham* and *Bride and Prejudice*, has opened up new horizons for the younger generation.

8

Festivals and Holidays

Let good conduct be thy fasting.

—Guru Nanak

Sikhism emerged and developed in the context of a rich multi-faith and multicultural environment. Sikhs celebrate many festivals that remind them of their history and connection to preindustrial Punjabi civilization. Most Sikh/Punjabi festivals originated in the pre-Sikh period and are a reminder of the Punjabi cultural heritage. They are also recorded in the traditional Indic/Hindu literature. Sikh/Punjabi festivals play a very important role in the nurturing of Sikh tradition and remain a central focus of the Sikh lifestyle both in India as well as in the diaspora.

THE CALENDAR

Most festivals in the Punjab mark the unfolding of the seasons, agricultural cycles, and religious observances and rites. These annual festivals may be grouped into four seasonal cycles: summer (April–June), monsoon (July–September), winter (October–January), and spring (February–March). Their dates are calculated according to a lunar calendar called the *Bikarmi Sammat* (associated with the name of the famous Hindu emperor Bikramjit; *Sammat* means era). A lunar calendar consists of twelve months and is based on the time it takes the moon to complete one series of its successive phases, which is approximately 29.5 solar days. One full cycle of the lunar phase from full moon to full moon makes up a lunar month. A month comes to an end on the day of the full moon and is called *Puranmashi* (*puran* means complete, *mashi* means month). It is celebrated as an auspicious day. In the past, many Punjabi Hindu and Sikh women observed a fast on *Puranmashi* and donated ritual food to their village *Brahmani*.

The new moon, called *masya*, divides the lunar month into two fortnights (two weeks). In the Punjab, the festival of *masya* is celebrated locally. For example, every month a large number of pilgrims visit the *gurdwara* at Taran Taran, only a few miles from the Golden Temple, to celebrate the festival of *masya*. Before entering the *gurdwara*, the pilgrims take a ritual bath in the temple reservoir. The dates of all festivals and fairs are calculated according to the lunar calendar, so that they do not occur on the same date each year.

In recent years, there has been debate among the Sikhs over the use of the *Bikrami* calendar. A section of the Sikh community has been campaigning to set up a Sikh calendar, called the *Nanakshahi* calendar, which begins in the year of Guru Nanak's birth in *Sammat* 535 (A.D. 1469). Although this was intended to resolve the problem of fixing permanent dates for Sikh festivals, it has added to the controversy regarding the so-called "correct" date. In fact, many festivals are celebrated on two dates depending on the choice of the management of the local *gurdwaras*. For example, according to the traditional calendar the festival of *Sangrand* in the month of *Magh* was on January 13, 2004, while it was listed on January 14, 2004, on the *Nanakshahi* calendar. Moreover, despite the introduction of a new calendar, the dates for the birth and martyrdom-day anniversary of the Sikh Gurus continue to change according to the traditional lunar calendar.

Sikh festivals fall into two main categories: *gurpurb* and *mela*. The term *gurpurb* is made up of two words: *gur*, short for "guru," and *purb*, which denotes a sacred or auspicious day. The term *gurpurb* is applied to anniversaries when Sikh gurus are remembered. There are four main *gurpurbs* celebrated by Sikhs throughout the world: these are the birthdays of Guru Nanak and Guru Gobind Singh, and the martyrdom-days of fifth Guru Arjun Dev and ninth Guru Teg Bahadur. Sikh scripture is at the center of all Sikh festivals. A *gurpurb* celebration begins with the *akhand-path* (unbroken reading of the Adi Granth) and concludes with congregational worship. *Langar* is served twenty-four hours a day during the *akhand-path*.

In India, *gurpurbs* are celebrated by taking Guru Granth Sahib in a procession through villages and towns, called *jaloos*. The Guru Granth Sahib is placed in a decorated *palki* (palanquin) carried by *sewadars* (volunteers). A procession is always led by five Sikhs in traditional clothes, who carry swords symbolizing *panj pyarey* (the five Sikhs originally initiated by tenth Guru

Gobind Singh in 1699). Members of the *sangat* march behind the *palki* singing hymns.

Martyrdom day of the fifth Guru, Arjun Dev, falls in the months of May and June. Local Sikh *sangats* set up *shabeels* (stalls) to offer cold soft drinks such as *sharbat*, a mixture of milk, sugar, and water; orange juice; and Coca Cola to the general public. People are politely asked by volunteers to share cold drinks as a mark of remembrance. In 2004, the Sikhs celebrated the four hundredth anniversary of the compilation and the installment of the Adi Granth in the Golden Temple in 1604.

Mela

Mela literally means a fair. Sikh *melas* are both religious and cultural celebrations. Sikhs share a common cultural heritage with Hindus and celebrate important Indic festivals such as *Diwali*, *Baisakhi*, and *Holi/Hola* but with a marked difference in content and style. It was the third Guru, Amar Das, who began to encourage Sikhs to gather at his headquarters on the major traditional festivals of *Baisakhi* and *Diwali*, instead of making offerings to the Hindu Brahmins. In fact, this was the beginning of a new and distinct Sikh community in the Punjab.

Sangrand

The first day of every month in the Indic lunar calendar is called *Sangrand*, which is the Punjabi version of the Sanskrit term *sangkrant*, denoting entrance of the sun into a new sign of the Zodiac. It also falls on the next day of the full moon, called *puranmashi*. On this day, Hindu Brahmins visit the homes of their clients in villages to announce the beginning of the new month and receive customary payment in kind, such as wheat and sugar.

Sangrand is regarded as an auspicious day. It is observed by holding special congregational services at the *gurdwaras* for ritual announcement of the name of the new month from the Adi Granth. Guru Arjun Dev composed the hymn of *Bara Maha* (literally, the hymn of twelve months). It comprises twelve hymns collectively called the *Bara Maha*. Each hymn illustrates symbolic meaning concerning the various stages of human life and the journey of the soul; while directing Sikhs to conform to a specific code of discipline during each month. Sikhs visit *gurdwaras* on this festival day before setting off to work. A special *ardas* is recited for the welfare of one's family and the whole of humankind during the new month. It is important to note that the festival of Baisakhi occurs at *Sangrand* in the month of Baisakh on the lunar calendar.

Baisakhi

The major spring festival is *Baisakhi*, which is named after the second month, *Baisakh*, of the Indic lunar calendar. This festival also marks the advent of the harvest. For the peasantry, it is a long-awaited celebration: the fields are covered with ripe crops—the reward for their hard labor throughout the year. The festival of *Baisakhi* has a special significance for the Sikh community. In 1699, the tenth Guru, Gobind Singh, established the institution of the *Khalsa* brotherhood on the day of *Baisakhi*, which is associated with regeneration and new life. The ritual of replacing the covering of the *nishan sahib* (Sikh flag) is performed as part of the *Baisakhi* celebrations. Most *gurdwaras* organize the ritual of the *amrit* ceremony for those who aspire to join the *Khalsa* brotherhood and adopt the most orthodox style of visible Sikh identity.

Baisakhi festivities are marked by organized team games: soccer, hockey, and kabadi. Displays of individual skill and strength are demonstrated by experts in the martial arts and wrestling. Traditional *bhangra* dancing is the climax of the *Baisakhi* festivities, and the dancers dress up in colorful Punjabi costumes, accompanied by Punjabi folk music and a *dhole* (a large double-edged drum).

Diwali

Diwali is popularly known as the festival of light. It is celebrated throughout northern India in autumn. The festival of *Diwali* is associated with the ancient story of Lord Rama, who was exiled for fourteen years. According to the tradition, residents of the town of Aujodhya illuminated their homes to celebrate the homecoming of their beloved prince, Lord Rama. Traditionally, earthen *divas* (small oil lamps) were used by the people. Apart from decorating their homes, village people place *divas* in the cremation ground as a mark of reverence for the pre-Aryan Indic god Siva. It is interesting to note that in Punjabi villages a cremation ground is called *siva*, which has close affinity with the name of Lord Siva, who is regarded as the god of *bhut/pret* (ghosts). The cremation ground (*siva*) is believed to be the abode of Lord Siva. According to A.L. Basham, "Lord Siva lurks in horrible places such as battlefields, burning [cremation] grounds and crossroads, which in India, as in Europe, were looked upon as very inauspicious. He wears a garland of skulls and is surrounded by ghosts, evil spirits and demons."[23]

The festival of *Diwali* is also associated with the Indic goddess Lakshmi, who is believed to be the bestower of good fortune and prosperity. The people usually thoroughly clean their houses and keep the doors open throughout the night in anticipation of a visit by Lakshmi.

During Diwali, gifts of Indian sweets are exchanged by friends and families. The commercial classes clear their old accounts and look to *Diwali* as the beginning of the new business year. It is also New Year's Day on the Indian calendar. Hindu craftsmen worship their tools on the following day, which is called *Vishvakarma Puja* (worship of Lord *Vishvakarma*, deity of Hindu craftsmen), or *Bhai-Dooj*. Many *Ramgarhia/Tarkhan* Sikh craftsmen also worship their tools and participate in the *Vishvakarma* Day celebrations.

The festival of *Diwali* has other significance for Sikhs. It is associated with release of the sixth Guru, Hargobind, from the Gowalior Fort, where he was imprisoned by the Mughal emperor Jehangir. According to Sikh tradition, sixth Guru Hargobind was imprisoned on a charge of treason because he raised an army to rise up against the Mughal rulers. However, the authorities found no concrete evidence for the charge and decided to release him. At that time, there were fifty-two other Hindu princes in the prison, and Guru Hargobind refused to leave prison without the release of the other Hindu princes. The authorities agreed to the Guru's demand and said, "We can release as many of them as can come out of the fort holding your garment and hands." [24] On hearing this, the Guru had a special garment prepared with fifty-two cloth-strips sewn around it. In this way, all the princes came out with the Guru. The Guru afterward became popularly known as the *Bandi Chord* (deliverer of prisoners).

The residents of Amritsar celebrated his arrival by illuminating the Golden Temple and their houses. Today, *gurdwaras* and houses are decorated with candles and rows of lights, and fireworks displays are organized as part of the celebrations, as in Amritsar. In Great Britain and elsewhere, diaspora Sikhs take Indian sweets to their local *gurdwaras* as part of their offerings, and the celebrations culminate in an evening *divan* (congregational service) and fireworks display.

Bhai-Dooj

The festival of *Bhai-Dooj* is celebrated by the craftsmen of India and Sri Lanka; it falls on the day following the festival of *Diwali*. On this day, the artisans worship their tools, a ritual popularly known as *sand raj bathalna* (placing tools on the throne). The tools are worshipped as a symbolic representation of the Indic deity of craftsmen, Lord *Vishvakarma* (literally, creator of the universe). Worship begins with a ritual bath by an artisan, who then cleans his workshop by sprinkling water and lighting incense. The tools are ritually cleaned and washed and then placed on a raised platform, and the artisan bows before them (an act of *matha tekna*) as before a deity. The tools are not used until recital of the *ardas* invoking Lord *Vishvakarma* and the distribution of *parshad* (blessed food).

In the Punjab, the festival of *Bhai-Dooj* has been declared a national holiday. Sikh craftsmen called *Ramgarhias* celebrate the festival by organizing the ritual reading of the Adi Granth at their *biradari* (caste) gurdwaras. The celebrations conclude with a communal meal (*langar*). It is interesting to note that Indian craftsmen, including Sikh artisans, celebrate the festival of *Bhai-Dooj* in the diaspora with great enthusiasm. Today, they have established their craft associations, called *Vishvakarma Sabhas*, in several towns in India and abroad.

Hola

The festival of *Hola* takes its name from the Indic festival of *Holi*. In fact, the annual festival cycle culminates with *Holi* in spring; it is joyously celebrated on the full-moon day (*puranmashi*) of the month Phagan (February–March) on the Indic calendar. The festival of *Holi* signifies the triumph of good over evil. The traditional story of Prahlad and Holika is remembered during the festival. People dance in the streets and sprinkle each other with red powder and colored water. According to the Sikh tradition, tenth Guru Gobind Singh disapproved of the nature of the *Holi* festival and regarded it as a wasteful exercise, so he introduced the tradition of *Hola*.

Let us examine the traditional festival of *Holi* to gain insight into the essence of the festival. *Holi* is the celebration of the color of spring in northern India. It falls during the month of *Phagan* (February–March), when crops are ready for harvesting. People celebrate the festival all day by throwing colored water and colored powder at each other irrespective of caste, gender, or age. It was common to drink plenty of homemade liquor and to enjoy folk dancing all day. People would light bonfires and distribute sweets to children and relatives. Unfortunately, some would use the festival as a pretext for sorting out family feuds and engage in physical violence, which sometimes resulted in serious injuries and even death, and they would end up wasting their hard-earned money in the courts.

The main focus of the festival is the traditional epic of King Harnakasha and his son Prahlad, who was a devotee of Lord Vishnu. It is believed that the king wanted his son to be burned alive for this devotion. The king had a sister named Holika, who had a magic cloth that was fire-resistant. She was told by the king to hold Prahlad tightly on her lap and sit in the fire so that he would die in the flames. It is believed that Holika could not bear to kill the child, so she quietly transferred the magic cloth onto Prahlad and was burned herself. She attained *mukti* (liberation) for her pious deed and is worshipped as a goddess. This is how the festival of *Holi* received its glorious title.

It is believed that Guru Gobind Singh summoned the Sikhs to his headquarters at Anandpur to celebrate the festival of *Holi* in an entirely different and dramatic way. He organized mock battles between two groups of Sikh volunteers and trained them in the martial arts, thereby giving them a new purpose in life. The title of the traditional festival was changed to *Hola.*

Hola is one of the most colorful festivals held at Anandpur every year. Bands of Sikhs display their skills in the traditional martial arts as part of a huge procession that marks the culmination of the festival. Sikhs come from all over India to join in the celebrations, which continue for several days. An interesting aspect of the celebrations is the presence of the various political parties of the Punjab, which hold public conferences during the *Hola* celebrations at Anandpur.

There are a number of traditional Indic festivals associated with the seasons throughout the year. The people in the villages worship the god Gugga during the rainy season, as the number of snakes increase during this time of the year. As part of the celebrations, groups of folk singers visit every household and receive ritual offerings. The festivities culminate with preparation of a traditional Punjabi dish, called *saimeeyan* (similar to vermicelli cooked in water), which is first offered to Gugga. Women take the dish of *saimeeyan* to a spot outside the village, where it is believed the snakes reside in the bushes. Afterwards, the dish of *saimeeyan* is collected by the Brahmin women as part of their ritual reward for serving the community.

In the month of *Asu* (October–November), the male ancestors on the patrilineal side, called *Jathera*, are worshipped by their descendants. It is customary to feed Brahmins on the anniversary of dead ancestors during this month, and the ritual feeding is called *saraddha*. Today, most Sikh families ritually feed five initiated Sikhs and make offerings of clothes and some cash at the *saraddha* ceremony. Many Sikh families visit their ancestral villages to pay homage to their *Jatheras*. It was customary for a newly married woman to visit and worship family *Jathera* as part of her smooth incorporation as a member of her husband's clan. Most families in the diaspora organize the reading of the Adi Granth at the *gurdwaras* and prepare *langar* (communal meal) for the *sangat* in the memory of their ancestors.

Vart (Ritual Fasting)

Ritual fasting is most popular in Punjabi culture and is mainly observed by women on various occasions. Many unmarried women observe the ritual fast in order to secure a good husband, and married women fast for the general welfare of their husbands. The *vart of karva chauth* is most popular among newly married women. It is observed to pray for the long life of a husband. It is customary for the parents to take presents and Indian sweets to their married daughters at the performance of the *vart of karva chauth*. It is one of the important post-wedding rituals that assists the newly married woman to settle down in her new and permanent household.

Rakhardi

The term *Rakhardi* literally means a wristband. *Rakhardi* is one of the most popular festivals in the Indic tradition and is also called *Raksha Bandhan* (tying a wristband to a brother's hand by a sister). It signifies the unique nature of the brother–sister relationship. The ceremonial tying of a wristband is a ritual reminder of a brother's obligation to protect his sister in all eventualities. Married women travel to their brothers to perform the ritual tying of *Rakhardi*, for which they receive some cash and clothes, which confirms the emotional nature of the bond between sister and brother. Today, the *Rakhardi* is sent by mail to brothers who live abroad and in distant towns.

The ritual of *Rakhardi* begins with a ceremonial offering of an Indian sweet called *ladoo* to the brother by the sister. In fact, she puts a portion of the *ladoo* in his mouth and then ties the wristband. When a *Rakhardi* is sent by mail, a few grains of sugar are placed in the envelope for the brother to eat before the ritual tying of a wristband. Today, the commercialization of rituals has added an extra flavor to the festivals. *Rakhardi* greeting cards, like Christmas cards, are most popular; they contain printed messages that highlight the emotional nature of the festival. Some greetings are composed and printed in poetic form expressing a sister's love for her brother. It is also common practice to receive *Rakhardi* from one's female cousin or an adopted sister.

Lohrdi

Lohrdi is a spring festival that falls a day before the *Sangrand* in the month of *Magh*, which takes place on January 13 or 14 of every year. The festival of *Lohrdi* is celebrated to mark the first birthday of a boy. The family distributes sweets and roasted peanuts among relatives, friends, and members of one's *biradari*. In the evening, a huge bonfire is lit to which the women of the *biradari* are invited to sing songs celebrating the birth of the boy. It is customary to cook rice pudding in sugar cane juice and *saag* (green mustard or cabbage) on this festival. Interestingly, both dishes are eaten on the following day, which is the *Sangrand* of the month of *Magh*.

The *Sangrand* of the month of *Magh* has special significance for Sikhs. They celebrate the festival of *Maghi*, which is associated with the martyrdom of forty Sikh volunteers popularly known as *muktey* (liberated). They are reverentially remembered during the ritual of the *ardas* (Sikh prayer). Their martyrdom symbolizes the sacred bond between a Sikh and his/her Guru. The episode of their sacrifice originated during the siege of Anandpur (1704) by the Mughal army. These forty Sikhs disowned Guru Gobind Singh in writing as their Guru. It is believed that the contents of their letter contained the following wording:

"*toon saada guru naheen tey aseen teyrey Sikh naheen*" (you are not our Guru and we are not your Sikh).

Guru Gobind Singh eventually left Anandpur but was chased by the Mughal army. The forty deserters went to their homes

RAKHARDI

The festival of *Rakhardi* (*Rakhi* in Hindi) celebrates the love and affection between brother and sister as a sacred bond. What follows is a twenty-first-century wish of a sister:

> DEAR BROTHER,
>
> Sending you this *Rakhi*
> with LOVE and APPRECIATION,
> for being a SUPERB BROTHER;
> Wishing you from my HEART
> a Life filled with
> HAPPINESS and SUCCESS.
> YOU'LL ALWAYS BE DEAR
> TO ME, BROTHER.

The following *rakhardi* (wristband) wish is from a commercial greeting card. At the front cover is printed:

> DEAR Brother

In the center is a beautiful picture of a *rakhardi* and underneath is printed:

> Remembering today with LOVE,
> how CARING and PROTECTIVE
> you've always been towards me.

On the back cover is printed a small picture of a *rakhardi* with the following message:

> The love between a brother
> and sister is a
> sacred bond.

and told their story to their families. One Sikh lady, popularly known as *Mai* (mother) *Bhago*, highly disapproved of their desertion of the Guru and went on to lead them to fight for their Guru. The deserters laid down their lives fighting the Mughal forces at a village called *Khidrana*, where their bodies were left lying around a large pond. Once it became night, Guru Gobind Singh, along with some of the Sikhs stationed nearby, went to the site of the battle and their bodies. It is said that one of them, named Mahan Singh, was still alive but seriously wounded. He asked the Guru for forgiveness and to destroy their letter of desertion. It is believed that the Guru had kept the letter with him, and he tore it up on the spot before Mahan Singh died. The Guru declared the forty *muktey* (liberated). The pond of *Khidrana* was also renamed by Guru Gobind Singh as *Muktsar* (literally, pond of liberation).

Every year on the first day of the month of *Magh*, Sikhs from all over India and abroad gather at *Muktsar* to commemorate the heroism of the forty martyrs and their leader, *Mai Bhago*, who displayed the exemplary qualities of a leader, and to honor her place in Sikh history.

9

Memories

As many a flower blossoms in wilderness,
And wasted its fragrance,
So through many births I have wandered.

—Kabirji, Gauri Rag

Sikh tradition stands as one of the most dynamic socioreligious movements in the history of humankind. It emerged and developed in fifteenth-century Punjab, and over the course of two hundred and fifty years it was crystallized into a well-organized militant force. In order to comprehend and gain insight into the processes of its development, it is essential to understand some of the defining moments in history that continue to shape Sikh beliefs and practices to this day. At the heart of Sikh tradition lies the creative intervention of the human Gurus and their teachings.

The origin of Sikh tradition coincides with the transition from Afghan to Mughal rule in northern India. Babur, the first Mughal emperor, invaded India in 1526. It is believed that Guru Nanak witnessed the slaughter of civilian Punjabi people at the hands of the Mughal army at Aimnabad. He denounced the invading army as a "marriage party of sin." Commenting on the social and political degeneration of society at that time, Guru Nanak said in the Adi Granth, "Kings are butchers: cruelty is their weapon. The sense of duty has taken wings and vanished. Falsehood reigns over the land as a veil of darkness."

It was during the reign of Babur's grandson, Emperor Akbar—who provided peace and prosperity for his vast empire—that a favorable environment for interaction between Hinduism and Islam was established, which, in turn, had a major impact on the development of the Sikh faith and its institutions. For example, third Guru Amar Das made the *langar* an integral part of Sikh tradition by insisting that whoever wanted to see him had first to accept his hospitality by eating with the disciples. Among the people who visited Guru Amar Das was Emperor Akbar, who was required to eat with the people before he met the Guru. Akbar was so impressed with the Guru's teachings and the practice of equality of humankind at Goindwal that he donated a large grant of land to the center. Royal patronage greatly impacted upon the rapid development of Sikh tradition.

It is important to note that the Golden Temple was erected on the same piece of land donated by Emperor Akbar to Guru Amar Das. According to Sikh tradition, Guru Arjun invited his Muslim friend Mian Mir to lay the foundation stone of the Golden Temple, which was completed in 1604. The Adi Granth was also finalized in 1604, and was ceremonially installed in the Golden Temple. Tradition has it that Emperor Akbar examined the contents of the scripture and was deeply impressed by the selection of compositions and the messages it contained. These episodes are reverently remembered by Sikhs as significant markers in the development of the Sikh tradition.

Emperor Akbar died in 1605 and was succeeded by his son Jehangir. Akbar's death resulted in a major change in the policy of the Mughal government toward the Sikhs. Jehangir was highly critical of the growing popularity of Guru Arjun among the people of the Punjab, perceiving him as a threat to his empire. In his diary he wrote, "I fully knew [Guru Arjun's] heresies, ... and I ordered that he should be put to death with torture."[25] Guru Arjun was arrested and taken to Lahore. One day, he was taken to the river Ravi to wash himself after being tortured. He was thrown into the river, and his body was never recovered. Sikhs throughout the world commemorate his death as a martyrdom day.

The death of Guru Arjun proved to be a defining moment for the Sikh movement. He symbolized everything that Guru Nanak and his successors stood for. The manner of his death stunned the Sikhs. His son Hargobind took over leadership of the Sikh movement. His response to the tragic death of his father was equally unique. He introduced the ideology of defense of one's faith, which resulted in a qualitative change in the future direction of the Sikh movement. He established the *Akal Takhat*, which was reserved for discussing the social and political issues confronting the movement. Collection of arms and training of Sikh soldiers emerged as an integral part of a Guru's traditional responsibilities. He moved his headquarters to the foothills of the Himalaya Mountains while his cousins took over control of the Golden Temple and indirectly challenged his authority.

After imprisoning his father, Shah Jahan, Aurangzeb established himself as emperor of India. Like his grandfather Jehangir,

Aurangzeb brutally opressed the Sikh movement. He also embarked upon the policy of forced conversion of Hindus to Islam. Guru Teg Bahadur disapproved of this government policy, for which he was arrested and publicly beheaded in Delhi in 1675. The Guru's execution and the manner of his death terrorized the residents of Delhi.

According to Sikh tradition, no one came forward to claim the Guru's body and severed head, and they drew back to avoid recognition for fear of persecution by the authorities. At that time, one could not distinguish a Sikh by appearance alone. One devotee of the Guru removed the headless body under cover of darkness and took it home. In order to avoid suspicion, he set his house on fire and thus cremated the body. Sometime that night, another Sikh quietly took the Guru's head to Anandpur, where it was ceremonially cremated by his son Gobind Rai (Gobind Singh), who took over leadership of the Sikhs.

After several years, Gobind Rai decided to radically transform the Sikh movement and prepare his disciples for the momentous task ahead. On the historic day of the festival of Baisakhi in 1699, the institution of the *Khalsa* was born. The founding of the *Khalsa* infused a new spirit in the people of the Punjab. A large number of the Guru's devotees became *amritdhari* (initiated) and were ready to sacrifice their lives for their leader. The presence of many armed Sikhs at Anandpur was perceived as a serious threat by the Hindu rulers of the hill states. They petitioned the Mughal forces for help, and the Guru was eventually forced to leave Anandpur.

The Guru's departure from Anandpur is one of the most tragic episodes in the history of the Sikh movement. He was hotly pursued and attacked. His two sons, along with a large number of Sikhs, were killed in a battle at a place called Chamkaur. His mother and two youngest sons were separated from the Guru's entourage and were captured by the Mughal governor of the area, who put them to death. Eventually, Guru Gobind Singh and some of his Sikhs moved to Nanded in Deccan in southern India.

THE SIKH EMPIRE

Mughal Emperor Aurangzeb died in 1707, which marked the beginning of the decline of the Mughal Empire. Guru Gobind Singh was fully aware of the political situation in the Punjab. In Nanded, he met one of his trusted devotees (Banda), who is popularly known as Banda Bahadur in Sikh tradition (the name *Bahadur* means brave). He was a genius and an accomplished military leader. Guru Gobind Singh sent him to the Punjab to lead the Sikhs against the Mughal forces. He gave Banda five arrows from his quiver, his own standard, and a battle drum. The Guru issued special *hukamnama* to the Sikhs, urging them to join Banda's forces. Soon after Banda's departure to Punjab, the Guru died in 1708.

By 1710, Banda had captured most of the Punjab and declared himself ruler of the Punjab. He had new coins bearing the names of Guru Nanak and Gobind Singh struck to mark the establishment of a Sikh state. On his royal seal, Banda had inscribed the *deg* (cauldron in the Guru's *langar*) and *teg* (the sword of the *Khalsa*). In 1716, Banda was arrested by the Mughal army. Along with his followers, he was taken to Delhi for execution. At that time, two Englishmen, John Surman and Edward Stephenson, were in attendance at the Mughal court. In a dispatch dated March 10, 1716, they described what they saw:

> The great Rebel Gooroo who has been for these twenty years so troublesome in the *subaship* of Lahore [Punjab] is at length taken with all his family and attendants by Abdus Samad Cawn [Khan], the *suba* of that province. Some days ago they entered the city laden with fetters, his whole attendants which were left alive being about seven hundred and eighty, all severally mounted on camels which were sent out for that purpose, besides about two thousand heads stuck upon poles, being those who died by the sword in battle. He was carried into the presence of the king, and from thence to a closed prison. He at present has his life prolonged with most of his mustadis [soldiers] in hope to get an

account of his treasure in the several parts of his kingdom and of those who assisted him, when afterwards he will be executed, for the rest there are a hundred each day beheaded. It is not a little remarkable with what patience they undergo their fate, and to the last it has not been found that one apostatized from this new formed religion.[26]

Banda was executed on June 19, 1716. Before execution, he was offered a pardon if he renounced his faith and accepted Islam. Upon his refusal to do so, his son was hacked to bits before his eyes. Although Banda's success was short-lived, it prepared the ground for the establishment of a Sikh state in the Punjab. Banda had ushered in a wave of political awakening among the Punjabi people.

After the death of Banda, the Mughal forces began a campaign of terror in the Punjab to exterminate the Sikhs. The emperor issued an edict to apprehend Sikhs wherever they were found. Most Sikh fighters left their villages and retreated to the hills and jungles. Left without a personal leader, they innovated the tradition of making decisions collectively at the festivals of *Diwali* and *Baisakhi* at the Golden Temple. These assemblies were known as the *Sarbat Khalsa*. A resolution approved at the meetings was treated as a *gurmata* (order of the Guru). Moreover, the appointment of *jathedars* (group leaders) was also confirmed at these meetings.

The Sikhs organized themselves into twelve armed bands, called *misls*, functioning under approved leadership. In 1746, nearly seven thousand Sikhs were killed and three thousand were taken prisoner and later executed in Lahore. The Sikhs remember this episode as the *ghallughara* (the holocaust). In 1762, more than thirty thousand Sikhs—including children, women, and old men—were killed by the Mughal army; this is remembered as the *Vada ghallughara* (big holocaust).

Despite the massacre of 1762, the Sikhs gained enough strength to capture Lahore in 1799 under the charismatic leadership of Ranjit Singh, who became the supreme ruler of the

Punjab. Ranjit Singh disbanded the Sikh *misls* and emerged as sovereign ruler of the Punjab. With the disbanding of the Sikh *misls*, the institution of the *Sarbat Khalsa* lost its authority. Ranjit Singh died in 1839, and within ten years of his death the Punjab was taken over by the British.

The fifty-year period of Sikh rule brought peace and prosperity to the Punjab, and the Sikh hierarchy became fabulously wealthy. Members of the Sikh ruling elite lived like the Mughals and virtually forgot the teachings of the Sikh Gurus. The challenge of changing fortunes in the postannexation period gave birth to a number of reform movements, such as the Namdhari and Nirankari Sikhs. The Namdhari movement played an important role in the national struggle for Indian independence.

SIKHISM UNDER BRITISH RULE
The annexation of the Punjab by the British, in 1849, had an unprecedented impact on the development of Sikh tradition. Like Ranjit Singh, the British brought the Golden Temple under their control. The Deputy Commissioner of Amritsar formulated the rules and regulations and appointed a committee of loyal Sikhs to carry on management of the Temple, and exercised de facto authority over Sikh affairs.

The British administration introduced new forms of communication and transportation, including the post office, the telegraph, treated roads, railways, the press, and a modern educational structure. The new educational system was focused on teaching English language and literature, as well as Western sciences and social studies. Colonial rule initiated a program of social transformation of Punjabi society. The Punjab became an integral part of the British Empire, which opened up enormous opportunities for Sikhs both within India and abroad. This is how the internal and external migration of Sikhs began.

The Western-style educational institutions produced a generation of Sikh elites who had aspirations to reform Sikh tradition so that it could cope with the challenges of modern education and technological developments in India. In the absence of central authority, the Sikh elites implicitly assumed the role of representing Sikh concerns to the authorities. Under their leadership, the Sikh community launched a peaceful campaign, popularly known as the Gurdwara Reform movement, to gain control of historical *gurdwaras* from the *mahants* (appointees of Sikh gurus), who had been misusing the *gurdwara* property and indulging in immoral activities. During this agitation, a large number of Sikh volunteers were sent to prison and some lost their lives. Interestingly, a number of Sikh volunteers from the United States and Canada traveled to the Punjab to take part in the struggle and were arrested and sent to prison.

Let us now look at some of the crucial events that greatly impacted Sikh-British relationships and the development of the Sikh tradition.

Massacre of Jallianwala Bagh, April 13, 1919

On the festival of *Baisakhi* in 1919, a large number of Sikhs gathered at the Golden Temple. After visiting the temple, many Sikhs went to attend a protest meeting in Jallianwala Bagh (*bagh* means garden in Punjabi), which had only one entrance. The authorities had been alarmed by the rising opposition to their policies and so intended to crush the agitation.

Without giving any warning to disperse, British General Reginald Dyer gave the order to fire after his soldiers had blocked the lone entrance so that no one could escape the garden. The dead numbered 379, and more than 2,000 were wounded on the spot. The overwhelming majority of the victims were Sikhs who had come to celebrate the festival of *Baisakhi* at the Golden Temple. The massacre generated strong feelings against the British authorities throughout India.

The Nankana Holocaust

The *gurdwara* at the birthplace of Guru Nanak was a most wealthy institution and was managed by a *mahant* named Narain Das. He lived in the *gurdwara* with a mistress and was known to invite prostitutes to dance on the sacred premises. Local Sikhs threatened to remove him by force. But the *mahant* was the loyal ally of the government, so he sought police protection and also hired about four hundred thugs to deal with the agitators.

In the early morning of February 20, 1921, a group of Sikh volunteers entered the *gurdwara*. Soon the gate of the *gurdwara* was closed and Narain Das' thugs attacked the Sikhs with swords and firearms. The dead and dying volunteers were then placed on a burning pile of logs and burned. By the time the police arrived, 130 men had been consumed by the flames. The news of this outrage spread throughout the Punjab, and large groups of volunteers began to march to Nankana. The senior government officers rushed there and handed over custody of the gurdwara to the Sikhs. Agitation for control of other historic *gurdwaras* continued for several years.

At last the Punjab government agreed to the demands of the Sikhs and passed the Punjab Gurdwara Act of 1925. Under this act, a central committee called the *Shiromani Gurdwara Parbandhak Committee* was constituted to manage all historical *gurdwaras* in the Punjab. The committee is composed of 175 members who are elected every five years by the Sikh electorate. The SGPC emerged as a sort of Sikh parliament, and its decisions are regarded as *gurmata* (literally, guru's intention).

One of the important results of the Punjab Gurdwara Act was how it defined a Sikh person for preparing voting lists. It states that a person shall be deemed a Sikh for registration as a voter if he makes the following declaration in a Government prescribed pro forma:

> I solemnly declare that I am a Sikh, that I believe in the Guru Granth Sahib, that I believe in the Ten Gurus and that I have no other religion.

Ironically, the above definition excluded all those Sikhs who believe in the continuity of the line of human gurus, such as Namdhari Sikhs, Nirankari Sikhs, and Radhasoami Sikhs.

POSTINDEPENDENT INDIA AND THE SIKHS

The Sikh community played a most important role in the struggle for the independence of India. They have also displayed a remarkable capacity in creating a modern and democratic India. Since independence, Sikhs have held very important positions in the Indian armed forces. Although the Sikh population comprises only about 2 percent of the Indian population, their impact on the social, economic, and political fortunes of India is enormous. In the 1980s, Giani Zail Singh became the first Sikh president of India, and at present India has a Sikh prime minister, Manmohan Singh.

The Sikh *sants* (holy men) have contributed extensively to the development of Sikh tradition in the post-Guru period. Some got involved in Sikh political affairs. As mentioned previously, in the 1980s, a charismatic Sant, Jarnail Singh Bhinderanwaley, emerged as a powerful religious/political leader in the Punjab. He launched his campaign for the establishment of *Khalistan* (an independent Sikh state) from the *Akal Takhat*. The Indian army attacked the *Akal Takhat* to arrest Bhinderanwaley and his associates. This action resulted in considerable loss of life among both Sikhs and soldiers, and the virtual destruction of the *Akal Takhat*.

The attack, called "Operation Bluestar," generated strong feelings of resentment and anger among Sikhs all over the world. Indira Gandhi, then prime minister of India, was soon thereafter assassinated by two of her Sikh bodyguards. Her death was followed by unprecedented anti-Sikh riots throughout India.

10

Sikhism in
the World Today

There are three values;
Feel good, be good, and do good.

—Yogi Bhajan

SIKHISM OUTSIDE THE PUNJAB

The presence of Sikh communities beyond the boundaries of the Punjab, particularly overseas, is a remarkable episode in the history of human relations and has taken place over the last hundred and fifty years. This story began with the collapse of the Sikh state and annexation of the Punjab by the British in 1849. The independent Punjab state became part of the mighty British Empire overnight. The establishment of this colonial rule in the Punjab was one of the determining factors that initiated the wave of Sikh migration. Moreover, the pattern of Sikh migration is closely linked with the so-called notion of the "freedom of movement" within the British Empire.

One of the important results of the Sepoy Mutiny of 1857 was that Sikh soldiers received preferential treatment by the British army for the role they played in helping to quell the rebellion. Thus, a large number of Sikh soldiers were recruited into the army, mainly drawn from the agricultural sections of Punjabi society, and popularly known as *Jats*. Sikh soldiers were entrusted to safeguard the interests of the British Empire both in India and abroad. In order to build cordial relationships with the Sikh community, the British approved one of the most radical regulations that assured the Sikh recruits that their tradition of *Khalsa* discipline would not be interfered with.

While serving in the armed forces, Sikh soldiers were able to gain personal knowledge about potential economic opportunities in various parts of the British Empire. Consequently, after demobilization, many settled in such places as Singapore, Hong Kong, and Malaya, where they served in the police force, as security guards, etc. Some managed to immigrate to Australia, Fiji, and Canada. These pioneer Sikh migrants were a major source of information for their relatives and friends in the Punjab, which resulted in a cascade of Sikh migration.

Consider the Canadian experience of Sikh migration. The development of a Canadian Sikh community began in the first decade of the twentieth century, when nearly five thousand Sikhs arrived in British Columbia between 1904 to 1907. The new arrivals were met with high levels of prejudice and discrimination. The notion of "freedom of movement" within the British Empire was exposed when the Canadian government passed the Immigration Act in 1907, restricting emigration from India.

The Sikh response to the ban and racial discrimination was sudden and dynamic. In 1907, they established the Khalsa Diwan Society in Vancouver to fight against racial oppression and immigration restrictions. One of the first tasks the Khalsa Diwan Society set out to accomplish was building the first *gurdwara* there, completed in 1909. This *gurdwara* became the social and religious center of the Sikhs and soon emerged as a rallying institution for affirming their identity as Punjabi Sikhs. In this initial period, the pioneer Sikh migrants faced a great deal of hatred, hostility, and discrimination.

During the next fifty years, there was virtually no primary migration of Sikhs into Canada, which resulted in binding the Sikh community into a more tightly knit and monolithic group. During this period, the Sikhs displayed a remarkable capacity for adaptation and compromise. For example, most Sikh migrants removed their outward symbols and became clean-shaven. They would attend the Sunday service at the *gurdwara* without covering their heads; though, interestingly, they had fixed pegs outside the congregation hall for hanging hats. In the 1960s, immigration restrictions were relaxed, which resulted in the arrival of new Sikh migrants from the Punjab, who were instrumental in imposing orthodox discipline on the pioneer Sikh leadership. Furthermore, Sikh migrants were allowed to bring their wives and children, which led to a restructuring of the Punjabi/Sikh community in Canada. Soon a number of new *gurdwaras* were constructed in Vancouver to meet the social and cultural needs of the rapidly growing Sikh community. The *gurdwaras* regularly were host to professional *ragis* (religious musicians) and preachers from the Punjab with a view to transmitting authentic Sikh culture.

Between 1902 and 1910, nearly five thousand Sikh migrants arrived in the United States. Most of them settled in the northern

Sacramento Valley of California, where they built the first U.S. *gurdwara* at Stockton in 1912. Apart from serving the Sikh community, this *gurdwara* became deeply involved in the Indian nationalist movement and developed into the center of the Ghadar (Revolution) Party in America.

These Sikh migrants intended to buy farmland in the Sacramento Valley and become independent farmers. The authorities denied them citizenship, though, so they automatically lost the right to buy land. They had no choice but to work on other people's farms at very disadvantaged terms. They also were not permitted to bring wives from the Punjab. According to California's miscegenation laws, these Punjabi Sikh migrants could marry only Hispanic women, because men and women applying to the county clerk for a marriage license had to be of the same race/color and had to look alike.

Consequently, most of the women Sikh migrants married were Mexican Catholics. Interestingly, only a few men converted to Catholicism. Almost all the men encouraged their children to be brought up as Christians, and they viewed this very positively. Their wives and children also attended various functions at the Stockton *gurdwara*. One mixed-race woman, Susanna Mesa Rodriguez Singh explained her experience of attending the Stockton *gurdwara*: "God gives a lot of different languages, you know, but I don't think so many Gods," and her husband Moola Singh affirmed, "Only one God." [27]

In the mid-1960s U.S. immigration rules were relaxed, and a significant number of Sikh urban professional migrants were allowed to enter the country. Their presence in big cities prompted the Sikhs to build *gurdwaras*, which became centers for social and religious nurturing of Sikh families in their new environments.

Migration to East Africa
The annexation of the Punjab also opened up new opportunities for Sikh craftsmen, popularly known as *Tarkhans* (carpenters,

blacksmiths, and bricklayers), both in India and abroad. The second-most important wave of migration from the Punjab was that of the Sikh craftsmen, also known as *Ramgarhias*, who ventured to East Africa in the early twentieth century. Their migration followed quite a different pattern. They were recruited as indentured labor to build the Uganda-Kenya Railway. Between 1897 and 1901, nearly 32,000 Indian workers were recruited from the Punjab. More skilled labor was subsequently recruited to fill middle-level roles in the colonial administration.

Migration of Sikh craftsmen to East Africa continued until 1950, with only some immigration restrictions. But as there were no restrictions on bringing spouses from the Punjab, a vibrant Sikh community developed there. By this time, many Sikhs were employed in banks, post offices, and the police force, and their children became teachers, doctors, lawyers, and accountants. Some of them became highly successful building contractors and owners of automobile garages throughout East Africa.

British rule in the Punjab had a dramatic impact on the social status of Punjabi Sikh craftsmen. Traditionally, they were known as *kamis* (low-caste), who worked for their *Jat* (land-owning caste) Sikh patrons. They were paid in kind twice a year. In East Africa they became industrial workers who received regular wages and had no ritual obligations to their employers. Their low-caste status of being a village *Tarkhan* had become outdated. Now the Sikh craftsmen began to assert their *Ramgarhia* Sikh identity by taking a leading role in establishing the first *gurdwara* in Nairobi in 1900. They also built their own caste-based *gurdwaras*, known as *Ramgarhia Board gurdwaras*, in the major towns of East Africa.

In the 1970s, most *Ramgarhia* Sikhs migrated to Great Britain as a result of the policy of Africanization in the East African countries, and they became actively involved in building caste-based *gurdwaras* in Great Britain.

Migration to Great Britain

Mass migration of Sikhs to Great Britain began in the 1950s, though a small number of pioneer Sikhs had immigrated there before the Second World War. They were mainly unskilled, single young men belonging to the agriculturist section of Punjabi society. There were no restrictions on the entry of British subjects and citizens of the New Commonwealth until passage of the Commonwealth Immigration Act of 1962, which controlled the entry of male migrants. But there were no restrictions on the entry of wives and children under eighteen years of age.

The main reasons for leaving India included pressure on land and scarcity of industrial jobs, combined with a shortage of unskilled labor in Great Britain. There was a boom in the British economy after the Second World War. Newly arrived migrants found jobs in the foundries and in the textile industry. Some 206,000 Sikhs immigrated to Great Britain during this period.

The arrival of families from the Punjab had a significant impact on the development of traditional cultural institutions in Great Britain. Before the arrival of families, Sikh migrants lived in male-dominated accommodations. A family required a larger and independent dwelling. In the earlier years of immigration, most families bought terraced houses near *gurdwaras*. The *gurdwaras* were the crucial centers for information and socialization for the newly arrived families. Most Sikh women started working in the clothing industry soon after their arrival. One of the reasons for going out to work was loneliness at home after children had gone to school. Going out of the home to work brought about a fundamental transformation in their traditional roles. Instead of simply being a housewife, they became creative members of the industrial workforce and earned a regular wage. As a result, they shared in the financial obligations with their husbands and steadily began to assert authority over the use of the family income.

Let us look at the experience of one Sikh woman who came to join her husband in 1966. She told us her story as follows:

I was a head teacher in a Middle School in India—I, along with my children, lived with our extended/joint family. I had no worries about my children who were properly looked after by other members of our household. Now my children went to school—I was on my own all day. I did not know anybody in the street. There was another Sikh family in the street but the lady went to work after her children had gone to school. All other families in our street were white and Afro-Caribbean.

Although I was literate in the English language, my spoken language was virtually non-existent. It made me feel totally isolated and helpless. A visit to the gurdwara on Sunday was most eagerly awaited where I used to feel at home. Soon I found a job as a machinist in a small clothing firm owned by a Sikh. I helped two English teachers who organized English classes for Sikh women. They encouraged me to attend short courses to work with young children in Play Group schemes. Soon I became confident enough to communicate in English and got a job as a nurse in a nursery school.

My children successfully completed their school education and went to university. This was the most worrying period in my life. They were growing up like Yorkshire children— their dominant language became English and they would question our traditional mores. Any hint of an arranged marriage was dismissed by them as an old-fashioned custom. As soon as they completed their university education and got jobs, they decided to get married to the spouses of their own choice. We were, I would say, informed rather than being consulted. It is very sad to see the increasing number of divorces among the Sikhs. Well! What can you do. Perhaps it is the Will of God.

In the 1960s and 1970s, a number of Sikh families set up their own businesses and some bought corner shops. A few families started sewing clothes at home for big firms and eventually set up their own firms. Most Sikh families moved

from terraced houses into semidetached and detached proper-
ties in the suburbs with a view to finding good schools for their
children.

The Emerging Second Generation

One of the most important developments within the Sikh
diaspora has been the emergence of Western-born and locally
educated second and third generations. Sikh parents regard the
education of their children as their most important investment.
Most Sikh youngsters, encouraged by their parents, follow a
strongly instrumental belief in education and usually choose
career-oriented courses. The presence of a significant number
of young male and female Sikh professionals has begun to
impact upon traditional Punjabi/Sikh cultural norms: they are
actively and creatively engaged in evolving new strategies to
organize their lives in the Sikh diaspora.

The Sikh community in the diaspora has displayed a remarkable capacity for adaptation and compromise. For example,
the traditional mode of arranged marriage has given way to
"assisted marriage." Now spouses are introduced to each other
and their consent is obtained before final approval of the
marriage. In many cases, boys and girls choose their spouses
prior to obtaining parental approval and virtually impose their
decision on their parents. Many parents feel as if they have lost
control over selection of spouses for their children, which had
been their exclusive privilege.

Although extended-family and friends' networks are a valuable
source for finding suitable spouses, matrimonial advertisements
are extensively used to meet suitable spouses, particularly from
one's caste group. For example, the editor of *Des Pardes*, a
Punjabi weekly newspaper published in London, claims: "More
than 3000 marriages are settled and performed through the
columns of *Des Pardes* in England, Europe, Canada, and US."[28]
Matrimonial advertisements provide deep insight into the
functioning of caste among Sikhs and the way they define their
Sikh/Punjabi identity in the diaspora.

Let us look at the matrimonial section of the May 14, 2004, issue of *Des Pardes*. Although the paper is printed in *Gurmukhi* script, its matrimonial section is in English, which is mainly aimed at the younger generation of the Sikh diaspora. There are thirty-four advertisements in this section, and their breakdown according to caste categorization is as follows:

Jat Sikh	22
Ramgarhia Sikh	4
Khatri/Arora Sikh	1
Khatri Sikh	2
Saini Sikh	2
Arora/Ahluwalia Sikh	1
Rajput (Goldsmith)	1
Sikh/Hindu	1
Ad-Dharmi	1

These advertisements provide insight into the process of cultural regeneration within second- and third-generation diaspora Sikhs. Let us take a close look at one of these advertisement:

Matrimonial correspondence required by respectable professional and highly educated Jat Sikh family for their Medical Doctor (MBCHB) daughter, currently working as a Senior House Officer. She is 26 years of age, 5'6" tall, slim, very beautiful, well cultured, and has an exceptionally well balanced personality. Ideal partner should be suitably professionally qualified (i.e. Doctor, Chartered Accountant, Lawyer, etc.) and from an educated family background, at least 5'10"+ tall, slim, clean shaven and cultured.[29]

It is evident from the structure of this advertisement that Sikhs regard caste as one of the important factors for the selection of spouses. Secondly, the requirement of a "clean-shaven" spouse challenges one of the fundamental requirements of Sikh orthodox identity. Furthermore, it is not only a public statement of their intention but a creative endeavor to invent a new form of visible identity by second/third-generation Sikh women. It also shows that these Sikh women prefer to postpone their so-called traditionally prescribed "right" age, usually between 18 and 21, for marriage. Another important factor is the acquisition of professional qualifications, which has enabled them to achieve economic independence. Although the advertisement seems to reflect the wishes of the Sikh parents, it is in fact what the Sikh women demand concerning selection of their partners, and implicitly extends the boundaries of gender equality within Sikh society.

There is a major shift in the nature of the Sikh congregations that regularly attend *gurdwaras*. Most of those attending are first-generation immigrants and couples living locally with their children. Punjabi is almost exclusively the language of discourse and of conversation among first-generation Sikhs, while school-age children converse in English. The overwhelming majority of the second and third generations are conspicuously absent from *gurdwaras*; though most make a special effort to attend family celebrations.

Sikh youngsters find *gurdwara* services boring because they are exclusively conducted in Punjabi, the language of the *gurbani*. The *granthis* and *ragis* are imported from the Punjab, and they have no understanding of the linguistic and cultural needs of Sikh youngsters. Sikh parents have begun to show concern about the appointment of bilingual *granthis* and *ragis* who could contribute effectively to spiritual nurturing of children by conducting some part of the service in English. There is no central authority in the Sikh diaspora to take up the issue of translating Sikh scriptures into modern English for the benefit of the second and third generations. Most *gurdwaras* import

Sikh literature, audio cassettes, and CDs of religious music from India that are displayed and sold on Sundays. There is an urgent need for literature that captures the experience and ambitions of diaspora Sikhs.

Occasionally, *gurdwara* leaders and *granthis* remark about the lack of interest in *gurdwara* attendance among youngsters. But there is no mechanism to encourage young men and women to participate in the management of *gurdwaras*. Today, the annual elections of management committees are conducted like parliament elections. Different groups field their own candidates, whose names and photographs are published in the Punjabi press. In many cases, the outcome of *gurdwara* elections results in creating conflict over leadership and splits in congregations that culminate in the founding of new *gurdwaras*. In some cases, physical force has been used and the police have had to intervene, and *gurdwara* funds have unfortunately been wasted on lawsuits. These incidents are widely reported in both the local press and the Punjabi press. The situation of tension and conflict deters second- and third-generation Sikhs from engaging in "gurdwara politics."

Most *gurdwaras* organize Punjabi classes for Sikh children because the parents want them to learn Punjabi so that they can read and understand Sikh scriptures. Some parents encourage their children to learn devotional music in order to perform *shabad-kirtan* at *gurdwaras*. During summer holidays, a number of *gurdwaras* organize weekly summer camps for children, where they are taught to conduct Sikh services, recite the *ardas*, and perform martial arts. The curriculum of summer camps is focused on promoting orthodox Sikh identity and teaching of the *gurbani*. Usually, the whole program is conducted in English and Punjabi.

The increasing number of *gurdwaras* in the Sikh diaspora demonstrates the Sikh community's resolve to maintain a distinctive identity. For example, the number of *gurdwaras* in the United Kingdom is more than two hundred and in Canada it is more than one hundred, while the number of *gurdwaras* in the United States is more than fifty.

Interfaith, Intercaste, and Interethnic Marriages

The subject of intercaste, interfaith, and interethnic marriage is regarded as most "shameful," a scar on a family's *izzat* (honor), bad luck for parents, and an extremely private matter that should not be discussed, shared, or divulged to outsiders. There is a social climate of "silence and denial" within the Sikh community with respect to marriages with "outsiders." In many instances, partners in such relationships have been ostracized by their parents. Despite the parental pressure, the number of mixed-race marriages is rising among Sikhs.

There has been a "reluctant" modification in the attitude of Sikh parents toward mixed-race relationships. Second- and third-generation Sikh graduates and professionals are at the forefront of this cultural transformation. Interestingly, a number of mixed-race marriages are conducted at the *gurdwaras*.

Process of Integration

The Sikh community in the diaspora has gone through many exciting as well as painful phases. By now, Sikhs have been living away from the Punjab for more than a hundred years. They have changed from single male economic migrants into settlers living in family households. They are no longer working purely as unskilled laborers, as there has been a significant shift in their employment and occupational patterns.

Although youngsters' commitment to their parental culture seems to be equally strong, their vision of Sikh traditional culture is quite different from that of the first-generation immigrants. Their attitude of questioning traditional values is generally perceived as a threat to parental authority, and some feel as if they have lost control over their children.

It is important to note that most Sikh parents regard the education of their children as a family investment and an instrument for enhancing their social status. A significant number of Sikh youngsters have gained professional qualifications—as doctors, dentists, lawyers, accountants, teachers, social workers, and nurses. The number of Sikh children attending institutions of higher education is growing rapidly.

The Sikh community has made special efforts to become an integral part of contemporary British society. The degree of integration can be measured by looking at the way the Sikh community is becoming part of the mainstream culture while retaining its distinctive identity. Although participation in *gurdwara* activities is a major attraction, many Sikhs are actively involved in mainstream politics. For example, a number of Sikhs have been elected local councilors and a few have been elected lord mayors. At present, there are two Sikh members of parliament in England and nearly half a dozen members of the Canadian Federal Parliament. Likewise, in 2000, Ujjal Singh Dosanjh became the first Sikh to hold the office of premier of British Columbia, Canada. He had previously served as the first Sikh attorney-general of British Columbia.

1469   Birth of Guru Nanak Dev, the first Guru.

1604   Compilation and installment of the Adi Granth in Harimandir (Golden Temple), Amritsar, India.

1606   Martyrdom of the fifth Guru, Arjun Dev.

1675   Martyrdom of the ninth Guru, Teg Bahadur.

1699   Founding of the *Khalsa* by the tenth Guru, Gobind Singh.

1708   Death of the tenth Guru, Gobind Singh, ending the line of human Gurus.

1710   Banda Bahadur occupies Sarhind and establishes the first Sikh state in the Punjab.

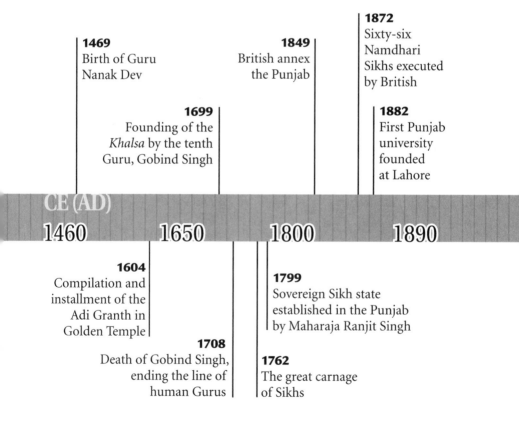

1469
Birth of Guru
Nanak Dev

1699
Founding of the
Khalsa by the tenth
Guru, Gobind Singh

1849
British annex
the Punjab

1872
Sixty-six
Namdhari
Sikhs executed
by British

1882
First Punjab
university
founded
at Lahore

CE (AD)

1460   1650   1800   1890

1604
Compilation and
installment of the
Adi Granth in
Golden Temple

1708
Death of Gobind Singh,
ending the line of
human Gurus

1799
Sovereign Sikh state
established in the Punjab
by Maharaja Ranjit Singh

1762
The great carnage
of Sikhs

1716 Banda Bahadur executed in Delhi.

1746 First carnage of the Sikhs (*ghallughara*).

1762 The great carnage of Sikhs (*Vada ghallughara*).

1799 Maharaja Ranjit Singh occupies Lahore and establishes a sovereign Sikh state in the Punjab.

1839 Death of Maharaja Ranjit Singh.

1849 British annexation of the Punjab.

1872 Sixty-six Namdhari Sikhs executed tied to the mouths of cannons; Namdhari guru Ram Singh deported to Burma.

1947
The Punjab is divided between India and the newly created nation of Pakistan

2004
Four hundredth anniversary of the compilation of the Adi Granth

1907
Khalsa Diwan Society established in Vancouver, Canada

1999
Sikhs celebrate three hundredth anniversary of the founding of the Khalsa

1910   1950   1980   2005

1912
First gurdwara established in Stockton, California

1966
Indian state of Punjab subdivided; Punjabi-speaking state is created with a Sikh majority population

1982
Giani Zail Singh becomes first Sikh president of India

1873 The first Singh Sabha founded in Amritsar.

1879 The second Singh Sabha founded in Lahore.

1882 The first Punjab university founded at Lahore.

1892 The first Khalsa college founded at Amritsar.

Late 1800s–
Early 1900s Punjabi/Sikh immigration to East Africa, the Far East, Canada, the United States, and the United Kingdom.

1900 First Singh Sabha gurdwara built at Nairobi, Kenya.

1907 The Khalsa Diwan Society established in Vancouver, Canada.

1909 The Anand Marriage Act legalizes Sikh wedding ceremony; first gurdwara built in Vancouver, Canada.

1911 First gurdwara established in London.

1912 First gurdwara established in Stockton, California.

1914 The *Kamagata Maru* docks in the port of Vancouver, with 346 Sikhs on board; forced to leave port on July 23; Canadian policeman William Hopkinson shot and killed by Mewa Singh, the *granthi* of the gurdwara; Mewa Singh sentenced to death; his martyrdom is celebrated every March in the Khalsa Society's gurdwara in Vancouver.

1919 Massacre at Jallianwala Bagh in Amritsar during the festival of Baisakhi.

1920 The Akali Party is established to free gurdwaras from corrupt *masands*, and the Shiromani Gurdwara Parbandhak Committee (SGPC) founded.

1924 A special *jatha* (literally, group) of five hundred Akalis approaching Jaito, India, is fired upon by police; three hundred Sikhs injured and one hundred killed.

1925 The Punjab Sikh Gurdwaras Act passed, which transfers control of the Punjab's historic gurdwaras to the

Shiromani Gurdwara Parbandhak Committee and provides an official definition of a Sikh person.

1926 Six *Babar* (literally, lion) revolutionary Akalis, are put to death by hanging.

1929 National Congress Party of India declares "complete independence" at their Lahore session; Namdhari guru Partap Singh is president of the reception committee.

1931 Bhagat Singh, Rajguru, and Sukhdev are convicted of murder of police inspector J.P. Saunders and executed; Bhagat Singh is popularly known as *Shaheedey Azam* (supreme martyr); Sikhs/Punjabis celebrate his martyrdom day every year throughout the world.

1940 Udham Singh hanged for killing Sir Michael O'Dwyer, who was the governor of the Punjab during the Jallianwala Bagh massacre.

1945 The *Rahit Maryada* (Sikh code of discipline) is approved by the Shiromani Gurdwara Parbandhak Committee.

1947 India gains independence from Britain; The Punjab is divided between India and the newly created nation of Pakistan; Sikhs flee to India while Punjabi Muslims flee to Pakistan; Many thousands killed in communal riots.

1950 The *Rahit Maryada* published.

1962 The Punjabi University inaugurated at Patiala, India.

1966 Indian state of Punjab subdivided, and the Punjabi-speaking state is created with a Sikh majority population.

1970 Sikhs leave East Africa to settle in the United Kingdom.

1982 Giani Zail Singh becomes the first Sikh president of India.

1984 Indian government launches "Operation Bluestar"; the Akal Takhat is destroyed and Sant Jarnail Singh Bhinderanwaley killed; Indian Prime Minister Indira Gandhi assassinated by her Sikh bodyguards; Sikhs are massacred in Delhi and some other cities.

1999   Sikhs celebrate three hundredth anniversary of the founding of the Khalsa.

2000   Ujjal Singh Dosanjh becomes the first Sikh premier of British Columbia, Canada.

2004   Manmohan Singh elected first Sikh prime minister of India; four hundredth anniversary of the compilation of the Adi Granth and its installment in the Harimandir Sahib (Golden Temple); Queen Elizabeth II attends; four hundredth anniversary celebrations of the compilation of the Adi Granth at a gurdwara in London.

CHAPTER 1:
Introduction

1 Sri Guru Granth Sahib (Adi Granth), 3rd ed. English and Punjabi translation in 8 volumes, translated by Manmohan Singh (Amritsar, India: The Shiromani Gurdwara Parbandhak Committee, 1989) 305–6.

2 *Rahit Maryada.*

3 Sardarni Premka Kaur, "Rejoinder," in the *Sikh Review*, XXI, 232, March 1973, 52–56.

CHAPTER 2:
Founders

4 Sri Guru Granth Sahib, 471–472.

CHAPTER 3:
Scriptures

5 Ibid., 628.

6 Ibid., 566.

7 Ibid., 19.

8 Ibid., 1,239

9 Ibid., 1,226.

10 Ibid., 39.

11 Ibid., 1429.

12 S.S. Kohli, *Sikhism and Guru Granth Sahib* (Delhi: National Book Shop, 1990), 114–20.

13 Ibid.

CHAPTER 4:
Worldview

14 Dasam Granth, 1,078.

15 Sri Guru Granth Sahib, 141.

16 Bhai Gurdas Var 20, *pauri* 10.

17 Ibid., 26.

18 Ibid., 992.

19 Ibid., 1.

CHAPTER 6:
Growing Up Sikh

20 Ibid., 963.

CHAPTER 7:
Cultural Expressions

21 From the standard *ardas* approved by the Supreme Management Committee of Gurdwaras.

22 Khushwant Singh, *A History of the Sikhs: 1839–1968*, vol. 2 (New Delhi: Oxford University Press, 1991), 179–180.

CHAPTER 8:
Festivals and Holidays

23 A.L. Basham, *The Wonder That Was India* (London: Fontana-Collins, 1967), 310.

24 W.O. Cole and P.S. Sambhi, *The Sikhs: Their Religious Beliefs and Practices* (Brighton, U.K.: Academic Press, 1995), 131.

CHAPTER 9:
Memories

25 Khushwant Singh, *A History of the Sikhs: 1469–1839*, vol. 1 (New Delhi: Princeton University Press, 1966), 60.

26 Ibid., 116.

CHAPTER 10:
Sikhism in the World Today

27 Karen Leonard, *Making Ethnic Choices: California's Punjabi Mexican Americans* (Philadelphia, Pa.: Temple University Press, 1989).

28 Matrimonial Section, *Des Pardes Weekly*, October 15, 2004, 54.

29 Ibid.

GLOSSARY

Adi Granth—Sacred scripture of the Sikhs, also called Guru Granth Sahib.

Akal—Timeless, a term used to describe God.

Akal Takhat—Literally the throne of the Timeless God; built by the sixth Guru, Hargobind, facing the Golden Temple in Amritsar.

akhand-path—Unbroken reading of the Adi Granth that takes forty-eight hours.

amrit—Nectar of immortality; solution of water used at the Sikh initiation ceremony.

amritdhari—An initiated Sikh.

anand karaj—The Sikh wedding ceremony.

ardas—Sikh prayer recited at the conclusion of a service.

Baba—Literally, a grandfather; a term of respect applied to holy men.

Baisakhi—New Year's Day in the Punjab, the first day of the month of Baisakh—one of the principal festivals of the Sikhs and anniversary of the founding of the Khalsa.

bani—Compositions of the Gurus and other saints included in the Sikh scriptures.

Bhai—Literally, brother, title of respect accorded to men of piety and learning; also used for the custodian of a gurdwara.

bichola—A matchmaker.

biradari—A Punjabi term that refers to both the brotherhood and members of a caste group.

charan pahul—Literally, foot initiation; water touched by the toe of the guru and used for the initiation ceremony; the Sikh method of initiation until it was replaced by the tenth Guru, Gobind Singh.

chauri—A ritual fan made of yak hair or peacock feathers; it is waved over the Adi Granth; symbol of authority.

Daan—Charitable gift for which no return is expected.

Daj—Dowry.

Dasam Granth—A collection of writings attributed to the tenth Guru, Gobind Singh.

dharmsala—A term commonly applied to a building used for devotional singing and worship; in the early Sikh period it was used to describe a Sikh place of worship.

Diwali—Festival of lights celebrated by Hindus and Sikhs in October–November.

Giani/Gyani—A person well-read in Sikh scriptures.

Granth—Book, a volume.

granthi—A Sikh who looks after the Adi Granth; a reader of the Adi Granth, may also be a custodian of a gurdwara.

gurmata—Literally a guru's intention; a resolution approved by the Sikh congregation in the presence of the Adi Granth.

gurmukh—Guru-oriented person.

gurmukhi—Literally, from the guru's mouth; script used for writing Punjabi; the Adi Granth is written in Gurmukhi script.

guru—Religious teacher or a preceptor; one who delivers a disciple from ignorance.

Guru Granth Sahib—Term used for the Adi Granth since the death of the tenth Guru, Gobind Singh, symbolising the end of human guruship.

havan—Fire worship; popular among the Namdhari Sikhs.

Hola—Sikh festival held at Anandpur.

hukamnama—A hymn read from the Adi Granth at the culmination of a service.

kachha/kachhahira—A pair of pants worn by the Sikhs; one of the Five Ks.

kangha—A small wooden comb, one of the Five Ks.

GLOSSARY

kanyadan—Gift of a virgin by her father.

kara—Steel bracelet worn on the right wrist, one of the Five Ks.

karah-parshad—Blessed food distributed at the culmination of a Sikh service.

Kaur—Literally a princess; name assumed by female Sikhs after initiation.

kes/kesh—Uncut hair, one of the Five Ks.

Khalsa—The Sikh Order instituted by the tenth Guru, Gobind Singh, in 1699.

Khanda—A double-edged sword, one of the Sikh emblems.

kirpan—A sword, one of the Five Ks.

Kirtan/shabad-kirtan—Singing of hymns from the Adi Granth.

langar—Communal meal served at the culmination of a Sikh service; also used for a kitchen attached to every gurdwara.

manmukh—A self-oriented person.

masands—Authorized leaders of local communities appointed by the Sikh Gurus before the founding of the Khalsa.

milni—Customary meeting of the heads of families before the wedding ceremony.

mona—Clean-shaven.

Namdhari—Literally, upholder of the Nam (God's name). A Sikh movement transformed by Guru Ram Singh; Namdhari Sikhs believe in a living guru.

nishan sahib—A Sikh flag.

Pag/pagri—A turban.

Panj kakaar—The Five Ks (wearing of the five emblems).

panj pyarey—The original members of the Khalsa; literally beloved five.

Panth—A term applied to Sikh society.

ragi—Literally a musician, a term used for the Sikh musicians.

Ramgarhia—A Sikh artisan caste that comprises carpenters, black-smiths, and bricklayers.

sahajdhari—A Sikh who may or may not wear outward symbols.

sangat—Sikh congregation.

Sat Sri Akal—Sikh greeting.

sewa—Voluntary service.

Shiromani Gurdwara Parbandhak Committee—The supreme management committee, which controls historic gurdwaras in the Punjab.

Sikh—Literally, a learner, a student or a disciple; a term used for members of the Sikh community.

Takhat—Literally a throne; a term used for five historic gurdwaras in India.

waheyguru—Wonderful Lord; a Sikh term for God.

BIBLIOGRAPHY

Barrier, N.G., and V.A. Dusenbery, eds. *The Sikh Diaspora: Migration and the Experience Beyond Punjab.* Delhi: Chanakya Publications, 1989.

Basham, A.L. *The Wonder That Was India.* London: Fontana-Collins, 1967.

Cole, W.O., and P.S. Sambhi. *The Sikhs: Their Religious Beliefs and Practices.* Brighton, U.K.: Academic Press, 1995.

Eleanor, N., and Gopinder Kaur. *Guru Nanak.* Alberta, Canada: Bayeux Arts incorporated, 1999.

Fenech, L.E. *Martyrdom in the Sikh Tradition.* New Delhi: Oxford University Press, 2000.

Grewal, J.S. *The Sikhs of the Punjab.* New Delhi: Cambridge University Press, 1999.

Kalsi, S.S. *The Evolution of a Sikh Community in Britain.* Department of Theology and Religious Studies, University of Leeds, 1992.

———. *Simple Guide to Sikhism.* Folkestone, Kent, U.K.: Global Books Limited, 1999.

Leonard, Karen. *Making Ethnic Choices: California's Punjabi Mexican Americans.* Philadelphia, Pa.: Temple University Press, 1994.

McLeod, W.H. *Sikhism.* London: Penguin Books, 1997.

Singh, Harbans. *Heritage of the Sikhs.* Delhi: Manohar Publications, 1985.

Singh, Khushwant. *A History of the Sikhs: 1469–1839.* Vol. 1. Princeton, N.J.: Princeton University Press, 1963.

———. *A History of the Sikhs: 1968.* Vol. 1. New Delhi: Oxford University Press, 1991.

Brown, Kerry. *Sikh Art and Literature.* New York: Routledge, 1999.

Sri Guru Granth Sahib (Adi Granth). 3rd ed. English and Punjabi translation in 8 volumes, translated by Manmohan Singh, Amritsar, India: The Shiromani Gurdwara Parbandhak Committee, 1989.

Joshi, L.M., ed. *Sikhism.* Patiala, India: Punjabi University, 1980.

Kohli, S.S. *Sikhism and Guru Granth Sahib.* Delhi: National Book Shop, 1990.

McLeod, W.H. *Who is a Sikh? The Problem of Sikh Identity.* Oxford, U.K.: Clarendon Press, 1989.

———, ed. and trans. *Textual Sources for the Study of Sikhism.* Manchester, U.K.: Manchester University, 1984.

Oberoi, Harjot. *The Construction of Religious Boundaries: Culture, Identity and Diversity in the Sikh Tradition.* Delhi: Oxford University Press, 1997.

Panikar, K.M. *A Survey of Indian History.* New Delhi: Asia Publishing House, 1971.

Singh, Harbans, ed. *The Encyclopedia of Sikhism.* 4 Vols. Patiala, India: Punjabi University, 1997.

Singh, Kashmir. *Law of Religious Institutions—Sikh Gurdwaras.* Amritsar, India: Guru Nanak Dev University, 1989.

Singh, Khushwant. *A History of the Sikhs: 1469–1839.* Vol. 1. Princeton, N.J.: Princeton University Press, 1963.

Singh, Pashaura. *The Guru Granth Sahib: Canon, Meaning, and Authority.* Oxford, U.K.: Oxford University Press, 2000.

———, and N.G. Barrier, eds. *Sikh Identity: Continuity and Change.* Delhi: Manohar Publications, 1999.

WEBSITES

Sikhism Information
http://www.info-sikh.com/

Information on the Sikh Nation
http://www.panthkhalsa.org/

News on Sikhism
http://www.sikhnet.com/

The Sikhism Homepage
http://www.sikhs.org/

Biography of Guru Nanak Dev
http://www.sikhs.org/guru1.htm

Sikh Photographs
http://www.sikhs.org/memories/

Sikh Advocate Organization
http://www.sikhwomen.com/

Sikhism Quotes, Articles
http://www.srigurugranthsahib.org/main.htm

INDEX

INDEX

God, 43–44
  and diversity, 41, 42–44
  and hukam, 49
  and karah-parshad, 62
  and Nam, 10, 12, 53
  names used for, 43
  oneness of, 4, 16, 18, 19, 32, 41,
    42, 43, 44, 50, 80
  and worship, 53
gogley, 71
Goindwal, 21, 106
Golden Temple (Harimandir), 4,
  13, 20, 22, 23, 34, 38, 42, 47, 48,
  54, 81, 82, 84, 87, 88, 95, 98,
  106–107, 110, 111, 112
gora (white) Sikhs, 13
government, and Sikhs, 114
Gowalior, 97
Granth Sahib, 32
granthis, 34, 35, 50, 55, 57, 61, 62,
  63, 68, 69, 77, 124, 125
Great Britain
  and Adi Granth, 34
  and childbirth, 66
  and craftsmen, 87
  and cultural expressions, 81–82
  and divorce, 75
  Indian independence from, 10, 67,
    114
  and Jat Sikh soldiers, 86
  and Namdhari movement, 10
  and naming, 67
  and Punjab, 7, 9, 29, 111–114, 116
  and Sikh soldiers, 116
  and Sikh tradition, 3
  Sikhs in, 120–122, 125, 127
  and turbans, 69
Greeks, 8, 9
Green Revolution, 87
growing up, 64–78
  and birth, 49, 50–51, 65–67
  and chhatti, 66–67
  and cremation, 76, 77
  and death, 49, 50–51, 76–78
  and family, 65

  and household, 65, 67, 77
  and inheritance, 65
  and naming, 3, 5, 6, 27, 67–68
  and pagri bananan, 68–69
  and patriarchy, 65, 66, 77
  and property, 65
  and widowhood, 76, 78.
  See also diet; marriage
Gugga, 100
gurbani, 31, 32, 33, 54, 61, 62, 124
Gurdwara Hazzor Sahib, 11
Gurdwara Kesgarh, 55
Gurdwara Reform movement, 112
Gurdwara Sis Ganj, 55
gurdwaras, 11, 20, 43, 46, 47, 47–48,
  53, 54, 55–56, 61, 67, 74, 78, 83,
  112, 112–113, 117–118, 119, 120,
  124–125, 126, 127
gurmata, 113
gurmukh, 43, 50
Gurmukhi, 21, 36, 39
gurpurbs, 94–95
gursikh, 6
Guru Granth Sahib, 10, 34–36, 94
Gur/u-mat, 3
gurus/guruship, 4
  and Adi Granth, 34–36
  definition of, 3
  institution of, 20, 32
  and Namdhari movement, 10,
    36, 47
  and Radhasoami movement, 12
guru-Sikh (teacher-disciple)-
  oriented movement, 3, 16
gusikh, 6
gutka, 53

hair
  and turbans, 3, 10, 13, 28, 68–69
  uncut, 5, 28
halal meat, 28, 73
Har Rai, 23
Harappa, 8
Harbhajan Singh Puri (Yogi Bhajan),
  13

144

INDEX

INDEX

CONTRIBUTORS

DR. SEWA SINGH KALSI is a lecturer in Sikh Studies at the School of Theology and Religious Studies at the University of Leeds, United Kingdom, where he specializes in teaching Sikhism and the development of the Sikh tradition in Great Britain. He is author of *The Evolution of a Sikh Community in Britain: Religious and Social Change among the Sikhs of Leeds and Bradford* (School of Theology and Religious Studies, University of Leeds, 1992), and *Simple Guide to Sikhism* (Global Books Ltd., 1999). He has also published many articles on the development of Sikh tradition in Great Britain. Dr. Kalsi was Senior Lecturer at Bradford and Ilkley Community College, where he taught South Asian Studies to undergraduate students. He has served on the International Editorial Board of the journal *Mortality* for several years.

ANN MARIE B. BAHR is Professor of Religious Studies at South Dakota State University. Her areas of teaching, research, and writing include World Religions, New Testament, Religion in American Culture, and the Middle East. Her articles have appeared in *Annual Editions: World Religions 03/04* (Guilford, Conn.: McGraw-Hill, 2003), *The Journal of Ecumenical Studies*, and *Covenant for a New Creation: Ethics, Religion and Public Policy* (Maryknoll, N.Y.: Orbis, 1991). Since 1999, she has authored a weekly newspaper column which analyzes the cultural significance of religious holidays. She has served as president of the Upper Midwest Region of the American Academy of Religion.

MARTIN E. MARTY, an ordained minister in the Evangelical Lutheran Church in America, is the Fairfax M. Cone Distinguished Service Professor Emeritus at the University of Chicago Divinity School, where he taught for thirty-five years. Marty has served as president of the American Academy of Religion, the American Society of Church History, and the American Catholic Historical Association, and was also a member of two U.S. presidential commissions. He is currently Senior Regent at St. Olaf College in Northfield, Minnesota. Marty has written more than fifty books, including the three-volume *Modern American Religion* (University of Chicago Press). His book *Righteous Empire* was a recipient of the National Book Award.